Understanding the Dynamics of the Value Chain

Understanding the Dynamics of the Value Chain

William D. Presutti, Jr. and
John Mawhinney

Understanding the Dynamics of the Value Chain

First published in 2013 by
Business Expert Press, LLC
222 East 46th Street, New York, NY 10017
www.businessexpertpress.com

ISBN-13: 9781953349033

ISBN-13: 978-1-60649-451-6 (e-book)

DOI 10.4128/9781606494516

Business Expert Press Supply and Operations Management collection

Collection ISSN: 2156-8189 (print)
Collection ISSN: 2156-8200 (electronic)

Cover design by Jonathan Pennell
Interior design by Exeter Premedia Services Private Ltd.,
Chennai, India

First edition: 2013

10 9 8 7 6 5 4 3 2 1

Abstract

The year was 1985. Michael Porter of the Harvard Business School published his business best-selling book, *Competitive Advantage*. It was touted at the time as "the most influential management book of the past quarter century." In that book, Porter introduced the concept of the value chain, described as "a systematic way of examining all activities a firm performs and how they interact, (necessary) for analyzing the sources of competitive advantage."

Looking back, the most significant and lasting contribution of Porter's value chain was the notion of interrelationships among a firm's many activities. It is the idea of "linkages," as he called them, which was the real breakthrough in management thinking. The linkages could be either horizontal among the activities inside the firm or vertical with constituents outside the firm including suppliers and customers. It was the firm and its outside constituencies and their respective value chains that formed what he called the value system in which all organizations operate.

Thinking of a firm as a series of horizontal and vertical linkages forced from out of the shadows the silo mentality within which firms operated and how business schools structured curriculum. That mentality caused all manners of organizational dysfunctions, including turf protection, anathema to the effective management of the value chain. The silo mentality also caused business schools to graduate students unable to see the firm as a holistic entity, an understanding of how all of its parts fit together to develop competitive advantage. Students were accounting majors, marketing majors, finance majors, and so forth, with little exposure to the importance of cross-discipline integration save for a strategic management course that most schools offer in the senior undergraduate year or as an MBA capstone. Students graduating with a silo mentality perpetuated the silo mentality in business firms. Unfortunately, that silo mentality continues to be all too common in businesses and in business schools.

Despite the need to help business professionals and students develop the holistic thinking critical to competing in the global economy, there are few comprehensive resources available from which they can draw. The purpose of this book is to help fill that void.

Fundamental to holistic thinking is a shift of mind, "metanoia" as Peter Senge called it in his 1990 book, *The Fifth Discipline*. This book is designed to draw together existing knowledge to help facilitate the shift of mind necessary to effectively manage the value chain. It introduces a new conception of the value chain, one that has been copyrighted (2006) and improves on Porter's groundbreading 1985 work, providing a new perspective of the value chain commensurate with the demands of the 21st-century global economy. The Porter model has not been updated since its introduction in 1985, yet continues to be used in current textbooks presenting the concept of the value chain.

Keywords

traditional value chain, contemporary value chain, dimensions of competitiveness, value chain management and profitability, required skills and abilities, reverse value chain, rethinking compensation practices

Contents

List of Illustrations

Acknowledgments

We thank Scott Eisenberg of CounselPub Publishing Services for the encouragement to write this book. Thanks also to Business Expert Press Collections editor, Johnny Rungtusanatham, for his invaluable input on content and flow. In addition, we thank our colleagues at Duquesne University's Palumbo-Donahue School of Business for their contributions. Dr. Ken Saban's input for Chapter 4 and Dr. Matt Drake's help with Chapter 6 are greatly appreciated. Dr. Kathryn Marley's manuscript review was especially helpful in clarifying key points in Chapter 2. Our thanks also to Mr. Darin Presutti for applying his expertise to assure the clarity of the book's illustrations. Finally thanks to Cindy Durand and Denver Harris of Business Expert Press for coordinating the editing and production process.

Introduction

This is a book about the transcendent issues that must be addressed if an organization is to create a value chain capable of responding to market needs. It is transcendent in the sense that it does not get into the technical details of managing the various components of a value chain. For example, if you are looking for guidance on how to manage inventories, or how to manage inbound and outbound logistics, or how to address queuing issues in operations, or how to deal with customer service issues, you will not find it here. There are many books and articles that exist for that purpose. Instead, we focus on the issues that we believe transcend the technical; issues if not addressed will render the technical ineffective.

This book will focus on issues not typically covered in any meaningful way in the existing value chain literature, issues like the nature and importance of cross-discipline integration and what happens if that is not achieved, the skills and abilities required of value chain participants and the explicit relationship that exists between the effective management of the value chain and an organization's competitiveness and profitability. It will also introduce a new conception of the value chain, one that we believe improves on Michael Porter's groundbreaking work in this area.

Although seminal, Porter's Value Chain model was introduced in 1985 and has not been appreciably updated since then. Yet, it continues to be used in the current management literature when the subject of the value chain is covered. The world has changed significantly in the past 28 years. Any work that seeks to create a model of the value chain should reflect those changes.

Managing a value chain requires that those participating in its activities possess the ability to think holistically. This is true from top to bottom in any organization for it is the integration of disciplines that is necessary if a value chain is to successfully convert customer needs to customer value. Therefore, in presenting the issues we believe are fundamental to effective value chain management, this book seeks to integrate concepts from a broad range of disciplines, developed over the past 100 years, including identity economics, organizational design, systems thinking, motivational theory, leadership, corporate and social responsibility and sustainability, and finance among others.

We hope you find the discussion of value chain management presented in this book useful whether you are a practicing business professional or a student seeking to expand your knowledge of the dynamics of this critically important concept.

CHAPTER 1

The Value Chain Revisited

Key Points

- A new value chain model that rests on a solid foundation of leadership, culture and people, appropriate infrastructure, and strategy
- The difference between the value chain and the supply chain
- Identifying external resources like an organization's suppliers as a key component of the value chain

Introduction

Michael Porter's seminal 1985 book, *Competitive Advantage*, introduced the concept of the value chain as a tool for analyzing organizations.[1] It was a breakthrough contribution to management thought because it stressed the importance of looking at the discrete activities a firm performs and how they interact to deliver value to the marketplace as a source of competitive advantage. Porter's generic value chain is very clear and straightforward. It has made a significant contribution to our understanding of how organizations ought to work to create competitive advantage. It continues to be influential in the academic and business literature.

However, it was published in 1985 and has not been revised since then. What we propose is a value chain model that reflects the changes in the business environment over the past 28 years.

We begin by providing a concise overview of the essence of Porter's generic value chain, identifying areas that we believe need to be revised. We then introduce a Contemporary Value Chain model that addresses fundamental areas of concern not addressed by Porter. The Contemporary model is designed to integrate existing thinking from various fields. Therefore, it exhibits the same concept of integration that the value chain itself requires to deliver competitive advantage. We identify key contributions of the Contemporary model and why we believe those contributions are important and consistent with the 21st-century business environment.

The Porter Model

Porter's value chain identifies nine generic activities broken down into four support activities and five primary activities (see Figure 1.1). The support activities include a firm's infrastructure, human resource management, technology development, and procurement. The primary activities include inbound logistics, operations, outbound logistics, marketing and sales, and customer service. A firm needs to realize a suitable margin from the activities it undertakes to deliver the product or service to the customer.

In addition, Porter set a firm's value chain as one (although key) element of a larger value system that includes the value chains of suppliers, distribution channel members, and customers. His value chain concept emphasizes the importance of linkages, horizontally among a firm's internal activities, and vertically among suppliers, channel members, and customers. He notes:

> The value chain is not a collection of independent activities but a system of interdependent activities. Value activities are related by linkages within the value chain. Linkages are relationships between the way one value activity is performed and the cost or performance of another.[2]

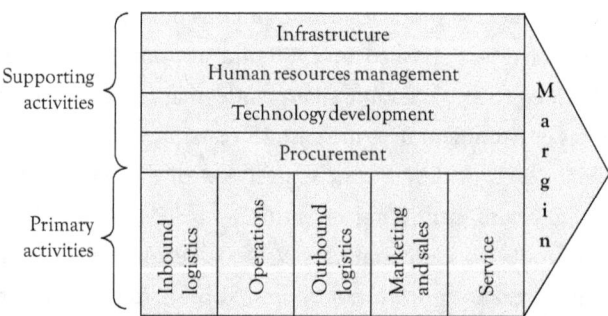

Figure 1.1. Michael Porter's value chain.

While that observation is on target, what is missing is the antecedent requirement of corporate culture that encourages, nourishes, and rewards the type of collaborative behavior that will promote value-creating linkages. This issue must be a fundamental consideration in establishing a highly effective value chain. Corporate culture underlies the human resource practices that Porter defines as a support activity in his model.

The Limitations of the Porter Model

The absence of a "culture" component is one limitation of the Porter model. There are some others. Since the mid-1980s, there have been radical changes in business thinking that have significant implications for any value chain model. For example, he identifies procurement as a "support activity" in his generic value chain. He notes:

> A given procurement activity can normally be associated with a specific value activity or activities which it supports, though often a purchasing department serves many value activities and purchasing policies firm-wide.[3]

With the development of the concept of supply chain management over the past decade, procurement, now more descriptively called supply management, is much more than a support activity. Rather, businesses look at supply management, through which more than 50% of their sales revenues flow in a goods-producing environment, as critical to competitive and financial success.

Sourcing decisions and total cost of ownership analyses are just two of the important activities in the field of supply management that will have a direct and significant impact on the firm's competitiveness and profitability. Therefore, rather than a support activity, supply management has transitioned over the past 15 years to be more properly viewed as a primary activity in a firm's value chain having a direct impact on the firm's ability to deliver value to the market. Several supply management experts have noted, "The discipline of acquiring and moving materials has become a key strategic advantage."[4]

Similarly, there are elements related to the other support activities that Porter identifies—technology development, human resource management, and infrastructure—that need to be viewed from a more robust perspective in a revised value chain model if it is to reflect contemporary reality.

More fundamental is the need to include the critical role of effective leadership as the foundation for effective value chain management and the need to identify the primacy of the customer, both not part of Porter's generic model. It is effective leadership that creates the culture of collaboration on which effective value chain management depends. Today, with shortened product life-cycle times, increasing global competition, and more demanding customers, the role of the customer needs to be made explicit in a Contemporary Value Chain model.

Finally, when one looks at the primary activities that Porter identifies in his model, they define what we now call the supply chain. The supply chain is an important component of the value chain but is not synonymous with it. Therefore, a newer model needs to reflect that fact of contemporary business.

The Contemporary Value Chain Model

The discussion that follows will explain our rationale and elements of a revised value chain model, one we believe is more consistent with the demands and challenges of business as we begin our journey into the 21st century. The model is designed to integrate existing thinking from various fields and to fill in the gaps we see in the Porter model (see Figure 1.2).

Leadership

We begin the discussion at the base of the value chain and work our way upward. Problems that firms experience in the marketplace result not so much from flawed strategies but from poor execution of those strategies.[5] The value chain, by virtue of the activities that it contains, is fundamental to effective execution.

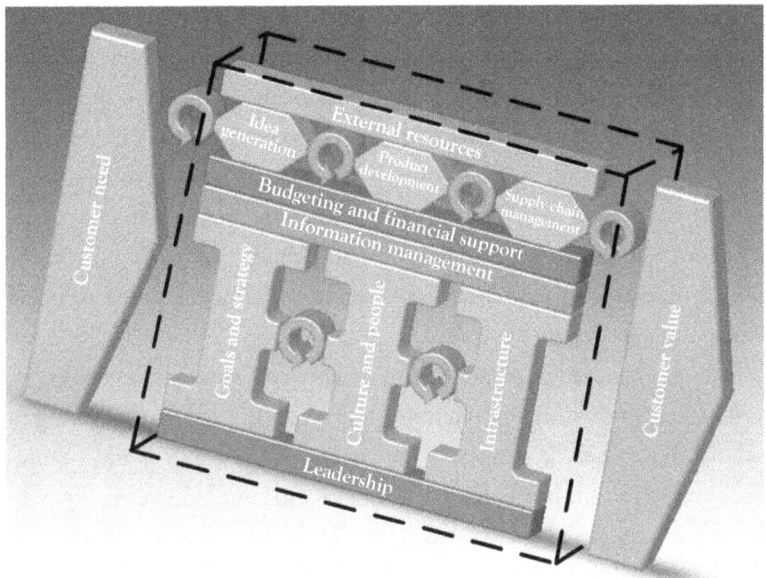

Figure 1.2. The Contemporary Value Chain.

Given the scope and linkages involved in the value chain, leaders must be able to grasp the value chain as a totality and understand how the interactions within it create value for customers. Mary Parker Follett, an important management thinker of the early 20th century, wrote about this important element of leadership.

Of the greatest importance is the ability to grasp a total situation … Out of the welter of facts, experience, desires, aims, the leader must find the unifying thread. He must see a whole, not a mere kaleidoscope of pieces. He must see the relation between all the different factors in a situation … My only thesis is that in the more progressively managed businesses there is a tendency for the control of a particular situation to go to the man with the largest knowledge of that situation, to him who can grasp and organize its essential elements, who understands its total significance, who can see it through—who can see length as well as breadth.[6]

Peter Senge's work on "the learning organization" is also relevant here.

In part, Senge identifies the role of the leader as someone "helping people see the big picture, promoting understanding of how different parts of the organization interact, and explaining how local actions have longer-term and broader impacts than local actors realize."[7]

It is not difficult to see what role leadership plays in managing the value chain for competitive advantage. Follett and Senge, while not writing about leadership as it relates to the value chain, effectively capture the essence of leadership in a firm that is serious about using the value chain concept to gain competitive advantage.

However, we do not want to convey the message that there exists an omnipotent individual on whose skills and abilities the functioning of an effective value chain rests. The concept of the value chain requires close collaboration horizontally in the organization and vertically with the firm's external constituents like suppliers. Therefore, leadership may be expected to be distributed among the participants in the value chain. This notion of leadership is what Mintzberg calls "community-ship." He notes,

> There is a need for more of what has been called distributed leadership, meaning that the role is fluid, shared by various people in the group according to their capabilities as conditions change.[8]

That is the type of leadership the value chain requires if it is to produce the dynamism essential to enable the firm to compete in an increasingly competitive global economy.

Let's now look at the three pillars built atop the base of effective leadership. They provide the support superstructure for an effective value chain. The three pillars include goals and strategies, culture and people, and infrastructure.

Goals and Strategies

A firm needs to be clear on how it intends to compete in the marketplace. Take, for example, four well-recognized dimensions of competitiveness—cost, response time, quality, and flexibility. A firm may choose to compete on one or a combination of those dimensions.

The dimension or dimensions chosen will dictate the basic design of the value chain.

If a firm chooses to compete on the basis of response time to market, then the value chain needs to be structured for speed. On the other hand, if a firm chooses to compete on all four dimensions simultaneously (a fair definition of a world-class competitor), the demands on the value chain are different. For example, Dell Computer Corporation built its reputation by competing on all four dimensions as we will discuss in Chapter 2.

Therefore, it is critical that the leadership identify goals that will enable customer need to be satisfied by the value created through the organization. Given these goals, effective strategies and business plans must be designed to achieve the desired results. This requires the leadership team to establish values and metrics that define the culture of the organization.

Culture and People

This is perhaps the most important pillar in the foundation of an effective value chain. Without a culture that encourages and nourishes collaboration and without people who are comfortable working in a collaborative environment, there is little chance that the "boundarylessness" characterizing effective value chain management will occur.[9]

McKinsey and company developed what has come to be known as the 7-S model to demonstrate the influence of corporate cultural values on a firm's activities. The model's management molecule establishes "superordinate goals" as the heart of the molecule. See Figure 1.3.

Those goals are another name for the values to which the company is committed and which impact all of the other elements of the model. For example, a fundamental corporate value that stresses the importance of internal harmony and cooperation will permeate the activities of all of the other elements. Let's use that value to understand the impact on the role of human resource management, a support activity in Porter's generic model, but in our model included with culture as one of the pillars of the Contemporary Value Chain model.

As the 7-S model indicates, superordinate goals impact the "skills" component of the molecule. The model defines "skills" as "distinctive capabilities of key personnel or the firm as a whole."[10] The corporate value

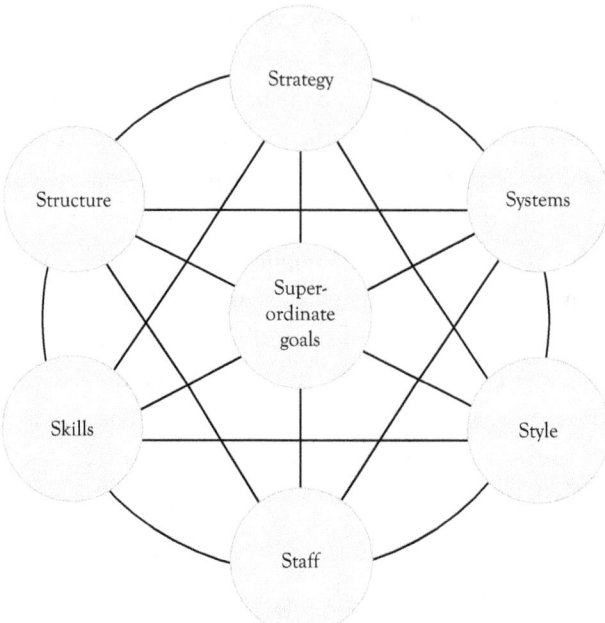

Figure 1.3. Applying the 7-S model.
Source: Pascale and Athos (1981).

of harmony and cooperation is fundamental to developing the linkages among activities essential for the functioning of a highly effective value chain. Therefore, it is incumbent on the human resource function and others involved in recruiting people to the firm that those recruited are predisposed to working collaboratively with their colleagues. Similarly, for those already on board, the human resource activity needs to provide developmental opportunities so that those skills can be acquired. Overall, the issue becomes one of personnel alignment, "getting the right people on the bus and the wrong people off the bus, and the right people in the right seats."[11]

The core value of harmony and cooperation will also impact a firm's systems. For example, the firm's performance appraisal system needs to include an explicit evaluation of a person's ability to work as part of a highly functioning team. Those that score well on this element should be rewarded accordingly. The organization needs to avoid what Steven Kerr calls "Rewarding A While Hoping for B."[12] Essentially, don't emphasize the importance of working in teams and then reward on the basis of individual performance measures only, hoping that needed teamwork will automatically occur.

The "culture and people" pillar of the Contemporary model is covered in more depth in Chapter 4.

Infrastructure

Infrastructure means the basic framework of the organization. It is comprised of four primary components that include organization, processes, technology, and facilities. Processes, technology, and facilities are enablers of the value proposition, providing the support to the people to efficiently and effectively execute the goals and strategies of the business. The integration of people, processes, and technology has become a major focus for those looking to improve productivity and service collaboration and virtual teaming.[13] The benefits of collaboration on a large scale require careful infrastructure design and maintenance. Strategies regarding infrastructure take on many shapes from those supporting stand-alone businesses to virtually integrated business alliances. Aligning the infrastructure to meet the operational needs of the business is essential to success.

A prime example of the interoperability of the Contemporary Value Chain model components is the securing of the infrastructure plank to support the rest of the model. Specifically, demands of organizations to manage information for all aspects of modern business are dependent on how well the people, processes, and technologies are integrated. Lacking the proper technology and processes to most effectively meet the customer's value needs can limit the competitiveness of the organization. These factors must also align with and support the organization if the greatest value is to be achieved.

Despite prognostications of the "the death of bureaucracy," most organizations today maintain the bureaucratic form.[14] There are individual departments of specialists, hierarchically formed, to carry on the daily work of the enterprise. Despite the efforts to "delayer" organizations over the past many years, the bureaucratic form remains. Firms have designed ways to ameliorate their rigidity including matrix designs and cross-functional teams that are formed and re-formed as the imperatives of the marketplace warrant. Overall, Alfred Chandler in his seminal work, *Strategy and Structure*, succinctly captured the role of infrastructure: "A company's strategy in time determines its structure and that the common denominator of structure and strategy has been the application of the enterprise's existing resources to market demands."[15]

In today's environment, how a firm's value chain is structured is determined by its strategy. In all cases, however, the structure must provide for linkages among functional silos and with the firm's external resources. That is the necessary characteristic for an effective value chain and one that is delivered through the structure of the firm's activities. In essence, we are describing a firm that is characterized by a high degree of boundarylessness.

An excellent example of this principle relates to the new product development process, one of the first key elements of our new value chain that emanates from customer demands. Boundarylessness helps to drive the design of a firm's infrastructure. The firm needs to be organized to facilitate cross-functional teaming. This approach to managing work flows from the cultural values of the organization and will depend on the skills and willingness of its people to work in that culture.

Figure 1.4 demonstrates the benefit of boundarylessness in the product development element of the new value chain. Situation A is the typical siloed organization where work is done sequentially. One department or activity completes its work and throws that work over the wall to the

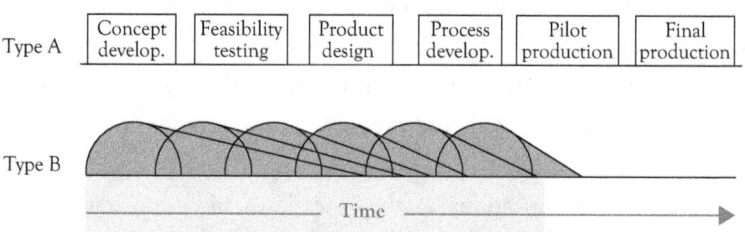

* Reconfiguring the product development
  activity in the value chain

Figure 1.4. The product development process.

Source: Adapted from Takeuchi and Nonaka (1986).

next department. When it gets to the production department for pilot production, only then do questions of manufacturability get raised with the likely result that the design would need to be revisited and reworked with the obvious negative implications on cost and time.

Situation B shows the benefits of a boundaryless organization where there is a significant amount of cross-functional involvement in the product development process from the beginning. The savings in time and cost are obvious. This approach becomes critical if a firm is competing on the basis of response time to market.

Fundamentally, the firm's culture provides the context in which an infrastructure dominated by a great deal of collaboration is both necessary and encouraged. The people, carefully selected to fit the culture, provide the firm with a competitive advantage through a tightly integrated value chain designed for delivering maximum value to the marketplace. A competitive advantage based on culture and the skills of the people is difficult for competitors to duplicate.

Resting across the three pillars of the Contemporary Value Chain are two important and pervasive beams that directly support the tangible value creating activities that allows a firm to transform "Customer Need" into "Customer Value." Those support beams are information management and budgeting and financial support.

Information Management

Information management is enabled by the people and infrastructure that provides a firm with the wherewithal to effectively and efficiently manage the value chain. Porter's generic value chain model recognizes the importance of technology development as a support activity. He explicitly identifies the importance of information management when he notes, "Information systems technology is particularly pervasive in the value chain, since every value activity creates and uses information."[16]

Porter's model includes a broad range of products, processes, and information technologies under the support activity of technology development. We choose to more specifically identify information management as a separate case that is pervasive and directly impacts the management of the value chain from suppliers to customers.

Information strategies that help to support supplier relationship management (SRM), enterprise resource planning (ERP), and customer relationship management (CRM) are clearly fundamental to managing the information needs of the value chain. What is of equal importance is that the interfaces enabled by the technologies provide a seamless integration that is much more common now than when Porter developed his generic model. More common then were technologies that were directed mainly at automating and integrating internally oriented applications for functional departments.

Today, with the rapid development of the internet and internet-based technologies, firms can seamlessly integrate internal and external functions through more comprehensive ERP systems and they can use information management and technology to improve existing business processes through business process reengineering efforts and create better relations with suppliers through SRM and customers through CRM.

It is this workflow software that has promoted the horizontal collaboration necessary to effectively manage the value chain. Workflow software is one of the fundamental flatteners enabling global relationships. As Friedman notes,

> For the world to get flat, all your internal departments—sales, marketing, manufacturing billing, and inventory—had to become interoperable, no matter what machines or software each of them was running. And for the world to get really flat, all your systems had to be interoperable with all the systems of any other company (suppliers and customers).[17]

As Figure 1.2 indicates, information management lies across the value chain's foundation pillars, suggesting its pervasiveness across the entire chain and can only effectively deliver value if the elements of the foundation permit. Take, for example, a company looking to reduce inventory through a vendor managed inventory (VMI) approach. VMI relies on information management technology to share inventory and sales information in order to control the flow and levels of inventory with the aid of suppliers. VMI can help overcome many problems related to inventory levels, such as poor inventory tracking, leading to higher levels of inventory, poor forecasting models leading to inventory deficiencies in case of unexpected demand, and a lack of trust between firms and their suppliers.

To illustrate, a consulting firm is hired to assess the impact of implementing VMI. It finds that the firm could realize significant cost savings. At this point, it is clear that the technology to enable VMI could deliver value for the company and contribute to more effective value chain management. The problem is that the infrastructure and culture were not compatible with what effective information management could deliver. The compensation for the vice president responsible for inventory is based on maintaining higher inventory levels. Regardless of the potential of the new information management system to help the company realize cost savings, this vice president is not willing to implement it.

The company is rewarding high levels of inventory while, at the same time, hoping for interdepartmental collaboration to reduce inventory levels to the point that they paid an outside consultant to evaluate the feasibility of VMI, a proven inventory-reducing strategy (a classic case of Kerr's admonition of "rewarding A while hoping for B"). In essence, the company was displaying one of the symptoms of value chain dysfunction, the suboptimization of organizational goals whereby one of the functions in the value chain puts its own goals ahead of the overall goals of the organization.[18] It was also clear that the company's reward structure was not consistent with an effective value chain management strategy. This issue will be discussed in Chapter 5.

Budgeting and Financial Support

Porter considers accounting and finance as part of the infrastructure in his generic model. As noted, earlier, we have defined infrastructure differently. We view budgeting and financial support as we view information management—a pervasive and indispensable force in the management of an effective and efficient value chain. The implication is that the firm's accounting professionals work closely with those in other disciplines to help facilitate the development and delivery of products and services that meet customer needs at a price the customer is willing to pay. Here the role of management accounting is indispensable. The results of the value-boosting actions of management accounting will directly impact resource allocation in the budgeting process.

Management accounting is typically viewed as an indispensable part of an organization's control system. It assesses the value chain's performance from the perspective of the organization's objectives. In addition to its assessment role, management accounting has an important role to play in directly managing the value chain starting with the product development and design process.

If one assumes that a firm uses market-driven opportunistic pricing, then management accounting will play an important role in assuring that a firm realizes a target profit margin from that pricing. That profit margin will occur if target (allowable) costs are met. In this process, and in the context of the value chain, management accounting identifies variances from the target costs to inform an improvement agenda, not simply to report variances from standard costs. The latter action does not encourage the type of continuous improvement thinking required for the management of a dynamic value chain.

Management accounting helps the product designers meet target costs by identifying variances from target, thus forcing redesign efforts through the process of value engineering.[19] In essence, for management accounting to be effective in supporting value chain activities, it must rise above the traditional focus on working within existing constraints and support a continuous improvement philosophy that believes there are no limits to improvement. That is a philosophy that all 21st-century value chains must be guided by to assure competitive success. Figure 1.5 captures the essence of this process.

Management accounting used in this way helps with the efficient allocation of resources that leads to value creation. For example, product designs may be value-engineered to eliminate unnecessary costs. This process helps the firm to develop more robust budgets that will not include the need to allocate any more resources than necessary for the product design in question.

The Contemporary Value Chain model considers finance to be a real driver of competitive advantage that permeates and enables the entire value chain; thus, its position in the model as a function is directly impacted by the way information is managed across the value chain.

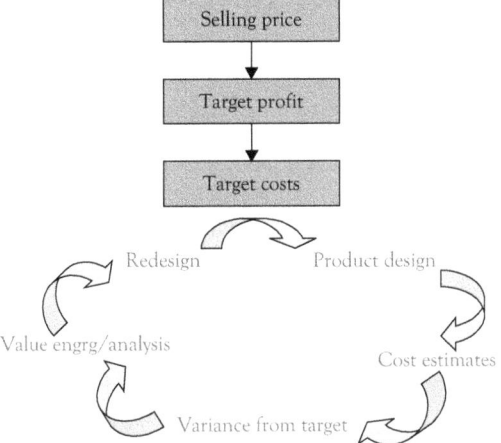

Figure 1.5. *Management accounting and value analysis.*

Given our ability to collect and analyze data today across business channels because of the advances in information management systems, finance can help us plan our strategic future, manage our operational present, and record our financial past in order to create value. The use of activity-based costing, target costing, and life-cycle costing among others can help a company make decisions and evaluate strategy. These tools will affect how all processes in the company are performed and, ultimately, will enable a company to create the most value possible.

Another important role of finance in the value chain is that it allows us to measure our financial success in delivering value to the marketplace. Figure 1.6 illustrates the use of economic value added (EVA) to connect different processes and activities in a company and their impact on the total value created.[20]

Figure 1.6 shows cost measures used in the supply management component of the supply chain as part of the total costs of supply chain management and, ultimately, a part of the entire company's costs. Those costs could include requisition costs and all costs associated with the purchase of goods such as receiving costs, invoice-processing costs, and so forth.

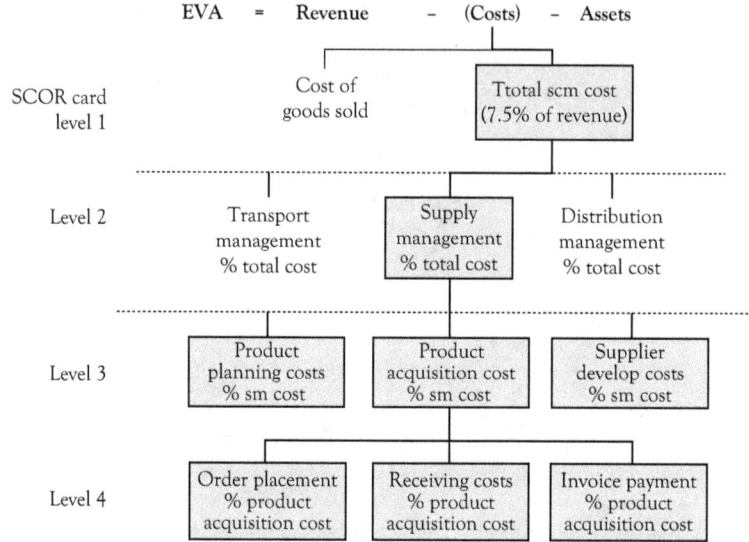

Figure 1.6. The impact of the supply chain on the cost element of economic value added.

This model allows us to pick the most important measurements and directly relate them to the overall measures used to understand the value added for the entire company.

Two perspectives are promoted here, both focused on value creation from value chain activities. First, an analysis can start at the top and find out where the higher costs are coming from and implement operational policies to control those costs or uncover cultural problems which are leading to those costs, and second, the analysis can start from the operational level to understand the impact of those activities on the total value created in the value chain. A more in-depth example is presented in Chapter 2.

Product Development

Moving to the top of the Contemporary Value Chain model, product development is the transformative process that converts an idea to a product or service that customers value. This process requires the collaboration of a number of constituents including marketing, engineering, production, supply management and suppliers depending on the industry, and actual final offering. Company culture and infrastructure are the two pillars of the model that play a significant role in the process.

A supportive culture is the necessary condition that promotes the interdepartmental collaboration essential for the effective product development. The culture, however, is not a sufficient condition. Infrastructure must be in place to facilitate the required collaboration. The siloed infrastructure must be supplanted by one designed to allow for permeability where turf is not protected and ideas flow freely among the relevant constituents. There is, therefore, a link among the product development, infrastructure, and culture components of the model as depicted in Figure 1.4.

For example, engineers must be open to recommendations by suppliers on basic inputs that may be more cost-effective without jeopardizing functionality. That requires close collaboration between engineering and supply management. In addition, product developers must be open to the design for manufacturability concerns of those in production. This pervasive collaboration between all relevant constituents in the value chain results in meeting three important dimensions of competitiveness—cost, quality, and response time to market.

As the need to revisit designs is eliminated, redundant costs are likewise eliminated and, as Figure 1.4 demonstrates, the time involved in product design is significantly reduced increasing speed to market. In addition, multiple inputs from various constituents with vested interests in the design (e.g., marketing, engineering, supply management, etc.) allowed by the infrastructure will most likely improve design quality if, by the right quality, we mean a design that allows all involved to meet their objectives, for example, marketing and customer acceptance, engineering and performance, supply management, and cost and availability of required materials, etc.

Supply Chain Management

As noted earlier, the primary activities in the Porter Value Chain model—inbound logistics, operations, outbound logistics, marketing and sales, and customer service—are important components of what we call today the supply chain. (Procurement, a support activity in the Porter model, is recognized as an important component of the supply chain on the input end of the Contemporary model and is identified as supply management.) The inbound logistics component of the Porter model is captured through the supply management and transportation components of the Contemporary model. Although Porter separates procurement from inbound logistics in his model, in practice, this is often difficult to do because effective supply management requires the careful planning of the movement of goods from suppliers to the buying company. The outbound logistics component in the Porter model is reflected in the distribution planning and transportation components of the Contemporary model. Once the primary activities are folded into the contemporary concept of the supply chain, Porter's graphic model of the value chain loses much of its conceptual foundation.

The Contemporary model takes these primary activities and consolidates them in the supply chain component of the model, allowing the model to include other elements fundamental to understanding value chain success, that is, converting customer needs to customer value. We do not show profit (margin in the Porter model) as an explicit element of the model because it is implied in a value chain that delivers customer value through competitive advantage and subsequent increases in market share.

Defining the Supply Chain

> Supply chain management involves proactively managing the two-way movement and coordination of goods, services, information and funds from raw materials through to end user … (requiring) the coordination of activities and flows that extend across boundaries.[21]

The definition of the supply chain begins with the concept of integration, fundamental to the effective management of the supply chain and the greater value chain of which it is a part. The concept of "flow" is also a significant element of the definition.

It is important to recognize that the integration of supply chain activities and the flow of materials, products, services, information, and cash takes place among both the firm's internal supply chain participants and its suppliers, thus the importance of the explicit recognition of "external resources" component of the Contemporary model. Overall, flow extends from a firm's suppliers to its customers. See Figure 1.7.

As Figure 1.7 suggests, the elements of the supply chain represent the "source–make–deliver" sequence required to link suppliers (source) with the internal components of the supply chain (make) ultimately delivering value to a firm's customers (deliver). All suppliers and customers are included in the "source–make–deliver" sequence. For example, an auto manufacturer may purchase dashboard assemblies from an assembly supplier who, in turn, purchases assembly components from its suppliers. The auto manufacturers make the final cars and deliver them to dealerships who sell to the final consumer. The "source–make–deliver" sequence applies to all companies either upstream (suppliers) or downstream (distributors) of the firm's value network.[22]

Any value chain model aspiring to describe the workings of the 21st-century value chain must clearly include a distinct supply chain

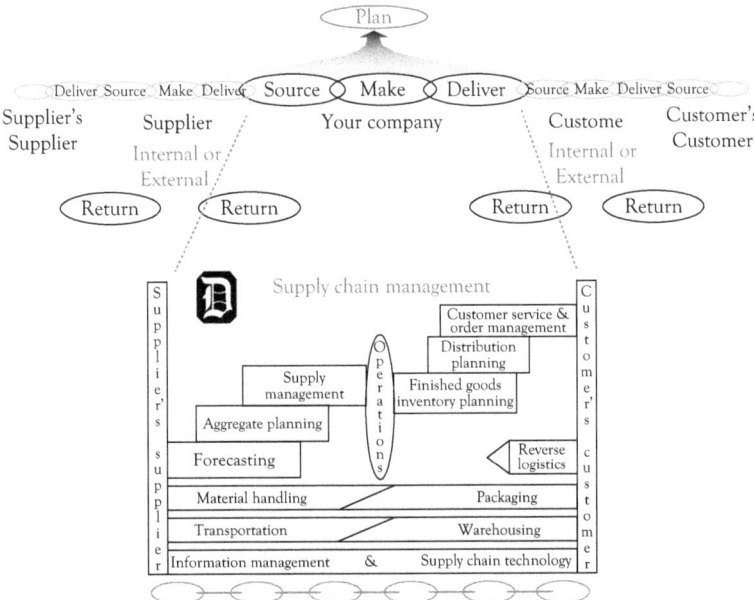

Figure 1.7. The basic elements of a supply chain.

Source: Mawhinney, J. Duquesne University Pittsburgh, PA.

element. An effectively functioning supply chain should deliver a competitive advantage to the firm because competition is no longer simply between companies but between those companies' supply chains.

External Resources

The final component in the Contemporary Value Chain model is "external resources." While Porter's concept of the value chain recognizes the importance of vertical linkages, external resources are not an explicit component of his model.

A firm's competitiveness in the 21st century depends on the quality of its external resources more than ever before. Friedman identifies 10 flatteners fundamental to his concept of the flat world. Four of them—outsourcing, offshoring, supply chaining, and insourcing—leverage external resources to improve a firm's global competitiveness.[23] In essence, a firm's external resources, a key element of which is its supplier base, is a fundamental part of its value chain.

Today, the firms with the best supplier base and who have cultivated productive relationships with those suppliers (developing vertical linkages according to Porter) will win the competitive race. As firms continue to pursue outsourcing strategies, the supplier base of the value chain becomes increasingly important.

Suppliers are not just depended upon to provide material, services, and equipment to support a competitive strategy but to contribute to the product development process. Effectively managed, supplier input at this stage of the value chain can help the buying firm reduce two important dimensions of competitiveness—cost and time—by 15–20%.[24]

Social Responsibility and the 21st-Century Value Chain

Inherent in the effective management of the 21st-century value chain is the concern for how a firm meets its responsibilities to the society of which it is a part. As concerns about the natural environment and global business practices mount, the success of a company will no longer be measured solely in economic terms, that is, profitability, but through the way it also meets its environmental and social obligations as well in what has come to be called the triple bottom line.[25]

This triple bottom line concern must permeate all activities in the value chain. Most important is that it must be explicitly recognized by the firm's leadership, permeate the corporate culture, be an important element of goals and strategies, and finally manifest itself in product development and actions in the supply chain including the decisions on the choice of suppliers.

For example, a major concern in product development should be the impact on the environment and the degree to which a product is recyclable through the reverse logistics process.[26] In the operations component of the supply chain, the issue should be if a product can be manufactured to minimize environmental impact. Here, if the value chain is being managed effectively, the importance of the internal integration between product development and operations becomes obvious.

Regarding suppliers, firms need to assure that social responsibility becomes an important component of the supplier selection process including issues like compliance with environmental regulations and, in the cases of offshore outsouring, child labor issues. In the Contemporary model, social responsibility is not considered a separate component but rather embedded in the very fabric of the value chain itself. We discuss this more in depth in Chapter 6.

Contributions and Significance of the Contemporary Model

We acknowledge Michael Porter's important and groundbreaking work on the concept of the value chain. Our effort here is to build on it and create a model more attuned to the 21st-century business environment.

First, including leadership as an explicit component of the Contemporary model reflects the fact that leadership matters as Jim Collins established in his book *Good to Great*.[27] Great leaders set the tone and are the foundation of a great value chain. Leadership is not an embedded feature of the Porter model. It needs to be made explicit that effective value chains just don't happen. They are effectively led and the tone of that leadership must permeate the organization.

Second, great leaders establish a corporate culture to allow great things to happen that create sustainable competitive advantage by creating value for the customer. Porter acknowledges the importance of both horizontal and vertical linkages among internal departments and external resources such as suppliers. However, the integration of functions and collaboration among them and with external resources necessary for effective supply chain management will be influenced positively or negatively by the corporate culture. A culture of collaboration is critical to success. It is not sufficient to identify the importance of linkages. Those linkages will only be productive in a culture that promotes values and rewards collaboration.

Likewise, Porter's model does not draw a link between culture and human resource management. He notes that "human resource management affects competitive advantage in any firm, through its role in determining the skills and motivation of employees and the cost of hiring and training. In some industries it holds the key to competitive advantage."[28]

However, he does not make a case for the link between culture and human resource management. The organization's culture will dictate (or should) the kinds of people to be recruited and hired, for example, those comfortable with collaboration. The culture also sets the context for the types of training and development offered and the types of compensation systems used, for example, individual versus group rewards.

Third, the dynamism of the 21st-century business environment is leading to ever-shorter product life cycles. Therefore, a more complete value chain model must include idea generation and product development as key components. Porter is silent on this point although he does discuss the importance of technology development in competitive advantage. Today, it is fundamental to competitiveness that the value chain begin with a dynamic idea-generation process and compressed product development cycles. Therefore, we include them in the Contemporary model.

Fourth, the Contemporary model calls specific attention to the fact that today's firm is an extended enterprise that depends on significant contributions from those outside the organization, most specifically suppliers, if it is to build a competitive advantage. Porter's concept of a value system, that is, the value chains of the firm and those of customers, channel members, and suppliers is akin to the notion of the extended enterprise. However, his model does not include a specific external resource component. Given the growth in outsourcing since his model's introduction, we believe that an up-to-date model needs to explicitly reflect this key development as an important characteristic of the 21st-century business environment. The external component lies atop the idea generation, product development, and supply chain components of the Contemporary model because firms need to draw on the expertise of suppliers in the early phases of the product development process. In the case of the supply chain, supply management plays an important strategic role in its interface with suppliers of materials and services, while logistics collaborates with transportation and distribution providers to execute delivery.

Fifth, the Contemporary model's supply chain component includes the primary activities of the Porter model including inbound logistics, outbound logistics, and operations and one of his supporting activities—procurement. Herein lies one of the most significant differences between the two models as explained earlier.

In today's business environment, with the typical goods-producing firm spending 50% or more of its sales dollars on the purchases of goods and services, and with the dramatic growth in outsourcing, there can be no justification for continuing to identify procurement as a support activity. The term itself does not adequately describe the evolution that has taken place in this increasingly important function in contemporary business. With responsibility for building supplier relationships and becoming more deeply involved with the strategy-planning process, procurement has evolved into "supply management." The supply chain component of the Contemporary Value Chain captures this change. Today, as business practice continues to evolve, the connotation of procurement itself becomes too narrow giving way to the more comprehensive supply management.

Sixth, we believe that no value chain model can be complete without an explicit recognition of the customer. As Peter Drucker postulated many years ago, "With respect to the definition of business purpose and business mission, there is only one ... focus, one starting point. It is the customer. The customer defines the business."[29] Therefore, the Contemporary Value Chain model starts with customer need and ends with customer value, denoting that the major purpose of the value chain is to deliver value to the customer.

Similarly, we also include goals and strategies as one of the foundation pillars of the Contemporary model based on the notion that the "customer defines the business." Goals and strategies call attention to the fact that elements of the value chain—principally the supply chain component—will need to be configured to serve the demands of a target market by delivering on one or more of the aforementioned dimensions of competitiveness (cost, quality, response time, and flexibility).

Although Porter addresses this issue as segment scope, it is not explicitly included in his model. We believe that any contemporary configuration of a value chain needs to demonstrate the role goals and strategies play because they will drive a value chain configuration to best serve the customer.

Finally, unlike the Porter model, we do not include "margin" in the Contemporary model. Porter defines margin as the difference between total value provided and the cost of activities that deliver value, that is, margin is created if what the customer is willing to pay (total value) is greater than the costs of creating that value. While it is obvious that a firm's value chain must create margin, we believe that it is a consequence of effective value chain leadership and management lying outside the construct of the value chain itself. Therefore, it is not included in the Contemporary model. In essence, we subscribe to Drucker's explanation of profitability: "Profit is not the explanation, cause, or rationale of business behavior and business decisions, but the test of their validity."[30]

Implications for Practitioners

We hope the Contemporary model is useful in helping practitioners recognize the antecedents required for managing a value chain that can lead to competitive advantage. Those antecedents include leadership, culture, and in Jim Collins' words, "getting the right people on the bus." It is also important for practitioners to appreciate the critical role that external resources play in delivering customer value. Too often, executive-level management is unaware of the connection between productive supplier relationships and company success. Therefore, they don't appreciate the value produced by the supply management component of the supply chain that not only contributes to competitive success but may boost profitability as well. Perhaps most fundamentally, the construct of the Contemporary model can help practitioners keep a focus on the customer as the beginning and end of what they do. For as Drucker argued, "any serious attempt to state what our business is must start with the customer, his realities, his situation, his behavior, his expectations, and his values."[31]

Conclusion

The Contemporary Value Chain model is designed to capture important elements of a firm's value chain that the Porter model does not. The Contemporary model builds on the important contribution of the basic idea of the value chain that Porter created 27 years ago.

The Contemporary model argues that the effective functioning of the value chain depends fundamentally on the quality of a firm's leadership, corporate culture, the quality of its people, and the congruence between the firm's strategy and its infrastructure.

The primary activities of the Porter model are consolidated into the supply chain component of the Contemporary model allowing the Contemporary model to include important elements not included in the Porter model, elements critical to an understanding and management of the 21st-century value chain including idea generation, product development, and an explicit recognition that a value chain cannot create value without collaboration with external resources. Perhaps, most fundamental is the need for a value chain model to include customer need as the driver and customer value as the outcome of value chain activities. This allows the casual observer to understand that the value chain has firm starting and ending points that are customer-focused, a critical consideration today for building competitive advantage. One does not get that sense when looking at the Porter model. The model itself has no customer component.

It also identifies what we believe to be the fundamental resources necessary for successful value chain management—people, budgeting and finances, information management, and external resources. Porter identifies the first three as support activities (human resource management, technology development, and infrastructure). There is no component for external resources in his model. The Contemporary model assumes that all of these resources are so deeply imbedded in the management of value chain activities that identifying them as support activities does not capture the essence of their importance. We have already made the case for including external resources in the Contemporary model.

Finally, inherent in the decisions made in the process of managing the Contemporary Value Chain is the pervasive notion of corporate social responsibility, an issue that has become fundamentally important in contemporary business. Overall, we believe the Contemporary Value Chain is a more complete and enabling view of the critical elements of today's business environment fundamental to delivering customer value and a template for strategic assessment of people, process, and technology integration.

This chapter is based on Presutti, W. D., Jr., & Mawhinney, J. R. (2009). The value chain revisited. *International Journal of Value Chain Management, 3*(2). Used with permission.

Suggested Actions

- Assure that leadership commands a holistic view of the organization.
- Build an organizational culture that emphasizes collaboration among value chain participants.
- Recruit into the organization only those who are comfortable working in a collaborative culture.

CHAPTER 2

The Value Chain's Impact on Competitiveness and Profitability

Key Points

- Deciding on how to compete based on four key dimensions of competitiveness—cost, quality, response time, and flexibility
- Value chain design and how it is based on the chosen dimension(s) of competitiveness
- The value chain–financial performance link and the impact on economic value added and return on invested capital

Introduction

Competitiveness and profitability—is anything more important to a business? Competition is more aggressive than ever in today's flat world.[1] It is being defined more as value chain versus value chain than company versus company. If Company A designs its value chain better than Company B, then Company A's chances of delivering on the value dimensions that customers demand increase. Customers will be willing to pay more for the value received than it costs for the company to deliver value resulting in heightened profitability. The value chain should be able to deliver sustainable competitive advantage leading to sustained profitability.

This chapter will discuss the key dimensions of competitiveness and the issues involved in designing a value chain based on the dimension or dimensions on which companies choose to compete. The impact of value chain activities on two significant indicators of financial success—economic value added (EVA) and return on invested capital (ROIC)—will be explained.

The Dimensions of Competitiveness

An effectively and efficiently managed value chain is a major key to competitive success. That success will ultimately lead to the company's profitability goals (see Figure 2.1). There are four core dimensions by which companies may choose to compete—cost, quality, response time, and flexibility. A company may choose to focus on one of those dimensions or may choose to compete on a mix or all of the dimensions simultaneously.

The first three are self-explanatory. Flexibility refers to the ability of a company to adjust to changes in customer demands. The four dimensions relate to Michael Porter's generally recognized strategies of cost leadership, differentiation, and focus, which serve as the basis for establishing competitive advantage.[2]

As noted, a company may choose to differentiate itself based on being a cost leader, speed to market, quality, flexibility, or any combination thereof. Or it may choose to focus on a market niche that places a high value on one of the core dimensions (beyond cost) for which customers are willing to pay a premium price. World-class companies can compete

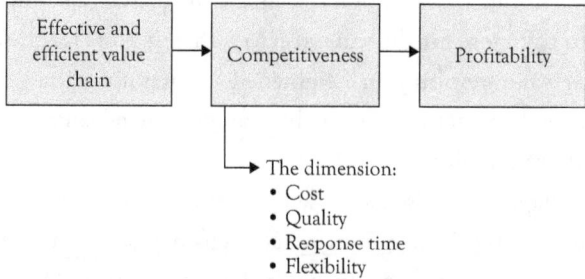

Figure 2.1. *Value chain management and competitive success.*

on all four dimensions. Dell Computer Corporation is a good example. Dell built its early success by:

- mass customizing computers based on customer preference (flexibility and quality);
- delivering a customized computer quickly (response time);
- offering customers superior value (they get to customize their computers) at a competitive cost.

Overall, Dell's value chain delivered value for which customers were willing to pay, helping it address the value equation:

$$V = p/c$$

where V = value, p = performance, and c = cost. Value is created for the customer when a company's value chain can lower a buyer's cost or raise the buyer's performance or, ideally, do both simultaneously.

A company may decide to pursue a focused strategy addressing the needs of a niche market. Consider this example. A circuit-board manufacturing company discovered that there was a niche market for prototype quantities of boards that were needed by design engineering departments of technology firms. Quantities were 25 units or less, significantly lower than the company's typical production runs of 500 boards or more. The customers' design engineering departments wanted high-quality prototypes delivered quickly and were willing to pay a premium price to get them. The circuit-board manufacturer set up a separate prototype production facility to meet this demand, charging customers a 25–50% premium price. The company established a competitive advantage based on quality and response time (the dimensions customers valued) and realized a significant increase in its profitability as a result.

Value Chain Design

Let us assume that a company sees an opportunity in the market to compete on the basis of response time. Today, speed to market is a critical competitive weapon. The significant components of the company's value chain must then be designed for speed. The starting point is at the beginning of the chain during the product-development process. That process must be configured (or reconfigured) for speed. As we saw in Figure 1.4 of Chapter 1, Situation A is the siloed organization. Beginning with concept development, each activity passes its work "over the wall" to the next, slowing down the process and extending the completion time. Worse, once the design gets to pilot production, those in charge of production may say "who developed this. We can't build it given the constraints of our production process." At that point, the process is essentially restarted while precious time to market gets longer and the basis for competing on response time is eroded.

Situation B solves this problem by promoting the use of cross-functional teams that tear down the silo walls. Important feedback is given early on and throughout the process helping to significantly reduce development time. The company needs to review all processes related to delivering fast response time to market eliminating or redesigning the value chain activities that slow down the process.

At the same time, the company's marketing intelligence indicates that with some well-targeted cost-cutting, competing on the basis of cost-leadership may also be possible providing added leverage to a fast response time capability. Attacking cost will enable marketing to use price as a competitive weapon without jeopardizing target profit margins. Therefore, the impediments to cost-cutting must be removed.

For example, an impediment may be in the value chain's supply management (procurement) function. Why? Because, in many cases, there has not been a differentiation between price and cost in the buying process. Those in supply may be predisposed to buy on the basis of low price so that they can report substantial savings at the end of the year to qualify for a bonus or whatever else is offered through the company's reward system. (Chapter 5 discusses the link between value chain management and a company's compensation structure.) Or, worse, those in supply do not understand the difference between price and cost. Of course, low price does not always result in low cost. However, in an environment where low price is rewarded, it is risky to pay a higher price for a purchased good because it may be difficult to explain (or demonstrate) to the uninitiated how the higher-priced product may be the best low-cost solution. Nevertheless, buying on the basis of low cost and not low price must become inherent in the company's approach to supply management.

Eliminating redundancies and inefficiencies improve response time capability. Well-targeted cost-cutting provides the foundation for pricing aggressively. The company is now in a position to boost its competitive position by competing on the basis of response time and cost. This is fully consistent with Porter's view that "a firm can achieve both cost leadership and differentiation simultaneously."[3]

Competitive advantage is built by providing value for customers through the company's impact on the customer's value chain. That impact is best manifested by recognizing that, as Porter notes, "value is created when a buyer's costs are lowered or performance raised."[4] In the example of response time and cost leadership, it is clear that a firm with a low-cost structure can offer lower prices to a customer, thus reducing the customer's cost of doing business while simultaneously getting the product to the customer faster. This allows the customer to respond more quickly and cost effectively to its downstream market—or minimizing on-hand inventory, thus providing additional cost benefits.

Overall, choosing the appropriate dimensions of competitiveness that allows the firm to exploit market opportunities is a necessary but an insufficient condition to maximize success. Issues about the capabilities of the value chain to deliver on those dimensions are equally important.

The Value Chain–Financial Performance Link

This section explores the critical link between value chain performance and business performance. Specifically, we demonstrate this link by explaining how the metrics of an important component of the value chain, the supply chain, can be coordinated and linked to corporate financial metrics. The supply chain performance metrics used are based on the Supply Chain Operations Reference Model (SCOR) developed by the Supply Chain Council.[5] The financial metrics are keyed to EVA, a widely accepted set of financial performance measures developed by the global consulting firm of

Stern Stewart and Co., and the more traditional ROIC.[6] Our conclusion: There is a clear and direct link between how effectively supply chain activities are executed and the financial performance of the business.

What the Literature Tells Us

Over the past few years, articles in the academic and business press have attempted to address the impact of supply chain management on corporate financial performance. Some have described the financial supply chain and the impact of effective supply chain management on a firm's cash flow. Others have considered the impact of just-in-time operations on financial performance, the relationship between total quality management practices and business performance, and the effect of supply chain disruptions on wealth. According to one article, "... any management actions must have an impact on key customer service dimensions, and it is this enhanced customer service that then engenders financial performance. Managers should not expect supply chain integration to directly impact a firm's financial performance."[7]

We take a different view. Using the Supply Chain Council's SCOR model, we propose that supply chain integration and specific related measures of supply chain performance have a direct impact on overall corporate financial performance. The supply chain metrics used by operating personnel focus attention on the day-to-day activities in the supply chain. By paying attention to the collective details of these daily activities, companies can boost their overall supply chain performance. And this, in turn, will be manifested through a positive impact on overall metrics of financial performance.

We are not alone in this assessment. A study by Deloitte Consulting of 600 companies in 22 countries concluded that the most effective firms have adopted a process view of their supply chains, rather than a functional view. "This end-to-end approach enables them to optimize the supply chain process across the entire organization and generate significant profit and returns," the Deloitte study found.[8] Put another way, effective supply chain integration has a significant impact on financial performance.

Performance Drivers and Outcomes

The linkage approach incorporating EVA and the SCOR model is really just another way of adopting the "balanced scorecard."[9] This tool identifies "performance drivers" and "outcome measures." The elements of the SCOR model are important supply chain–related performance drivers, while the corporate performance metrics represent important outcomes. Understanding the link between objectives and outcome measures is fundamental to achieving improved financial performance.

With that distinction between performance drivers and outcomes measures in mind, it is helpful to explain EVA and the SCOR model in a bit more detail. EVA is recognized as a comprehensive measure of value creation. In the words of one analyst, EVA "provides a more comprehensive measure of profitability than traditional measures because it indicates how well a firm has performed in relation to the amount of capital employed. It is expressed as "Net Operating Profit after taxes less the cost of capital."[10]

EVA emphasizes and isolates activities that help to drive value creation. These activities may be generally categorized as revenue, costs, and assets (see Figure 2.2). By understanding the EVA drivers, managers become more aware of the impact of innovation, cost reductions, technology improvements, and capital base reductions on value creation. As such, the EVA drivers align nicely with the performance drivers in the supply chain.

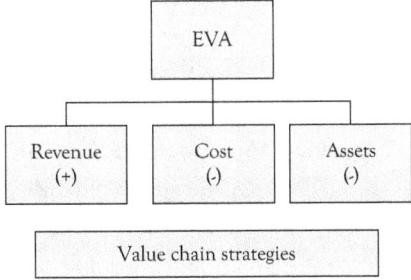

Figure 2.2. Economic value added elements.

An EVA orientation forces a firm to define its supply chain broadly. Thus, the definition will not only include the traditional activities like purchasing and inventory management with their obvious impacts on costs and assets, but also upstream activities like product design that may impact EVA's revenue element. Aberdeen Group, for example, found that integrating the firm's product development efforts with a supplier's engineering department through e-design technology may reduce time-to-market cycles by 10–15%.[11] In addition, this real-time collaboration may contribute to cost reductions by minimizing redesign time and uncovering opportunities for standardization. Since response time to market and cost control are key factors in market success, effective supply chain management at the input end of the chain may help to boost a firm's revenue through larger market share while lowering costs—two key elements in improving EVA.

The actions that can improve the profitability and value creation in the supply chain are generally under the firm's control. Better management of the supply chain should have a major impact on revenue growth, cost reduction, and asset turnover. The cost of capital is a different story, however: It is determined by outside forces and is essentially a given over which management has little control. Therefore, one of the keys to boost EVA is for the firm to efficiently and effectively manage its supply chain.

The SCOR Model

The Supply Chain Council's SCOR model can bring a measure of organization to the supply chain management measurement process and provide the link to overall corporate performance. The model identifies the need for corporate-level objectives, strategies, and business plans as the starting point for identifying best practice processes, concepts, and tools as well as selecting appropriate metrics. As such, it helps to overcome the disconnect between the supply chain metrics and overall corporate performance.

While the SCOR model is a useful tool through which the direct connection between supply chain management and overall financial performance could be demonstrated, the model itself does not make that connection. Instead, the SCOR model focuses on the hierarchy of planning and business goals, with requirements for objectives, strategies, and metrics at multiple levels in the business structure.

Figure 2.3 contains an important element of the SCOR model—the Level 1 "Strategic Performance Metrics," which are the strategic supply chain metrics. These metrics include performance attributes that have a direct impact on the customer (customer facing) and the firm (internal facing). SCOR emphasizes the need to continuously focus metrics on the requirements at the next higher level in the process to ensure continuity and support for corporate competitive performance targets.

For example, as Figure 2.3 notes, a Level 1 supply chain objective consistent with customer needs is "perfect order fulfillment" (reliability in delivery performance). Examples of objectives to support "perfect order fulfillment" are "on time delivery in full" and "orders shipped to schedule." A key performance criterion for industrial buyers is reliable delivery performance. High performance here can help the selling firm establish a competitive advantage leading to increases in revenue by capturing market share. As such, this result will have an impact on the revenue component of EVA. The internal facing Level 1 metric shown in Figure 2.3 impacts the cost and asset components of EVA.

SCOR level 1–strategic supply-chain metrics	Performance attributes					
	Customer-facing			Internal-facing		
	Reliability	Responsiveness	Flexibility	Cost	Assets	
Perfect order fulfillment	▤					R E V E N U E
Order fulfillment cycle time		▤				
Upside supply-chain flexibility			▤			
Upside supply-chain adaptability			▤			
Downside supply-chain adaptability			▤			
Supply chain management cost				▤		C O S T
Cost of goods sold				▤		
Cash-to-cash cycle time					▤	A S S E T S
Return on supply chain fixed assets					▤	
Return on working capital					▤	

Figure 2.3. Strategic performance metrics.

Source: Adapted from the Supply Chain Council.

Linkages in Action

The examples that follow demonstrate how the SCOR supply chain metrics can be coordinated and linked to support EVA. While the political and change management issues associated with internal multi-disciplined or multi-enterprise approaches are not addressed, it is important to recognize that those issues do exist and must be considered. The process described for establishing the SCOR model structure, especially when applied by cross-functional teams, provides for logically sound development of linked initiatives. This inclusive approach goes a long way toward overcoming resistance from both inside and outside the organization.

Using EVA as the measure of overall financial performance, the ties that the SCOR model process provides for linking the supply chain metrics to corporate financial goals are demonstrated. The focus is on the components of EVA typically under the firm's control—revenue, costs, and assets.

The Revenue Component

Starting with the development of the supply chain management (SCM) objectives and strategies, Figure 2.4 shows the relationship between the SCOR model metrics and the revenue component of EVA for a hypothetical company. One strategy for increasing revenue is to improve customer satisfaction. The SCOR model provides the process to prioritize and select the most significant supply chain support strategies and performance indicators to achieve this goal. For example, as noted earlier, one of the SCOR model's key attributes is "perfect order fulfillment." This attribute is typically a highly ranked customer satisfaction parameter on customer service surveys.

Perfect order fulfillment has many components. Therefore, a decision must be made on the appropriate second-level supporting metric. A metric in this sample company is "on-time, in full," which is critical in industries operating in a just-in-time environment. The number of processes that support "on-time, in full" can prove to be significant. For illustration purposes, let us continue the decomposition process to Level 3 to ensure that the efforts of those who impact the Level 1 perfect order fulfillment goal are properly focused. In these cases, one of the Level 3

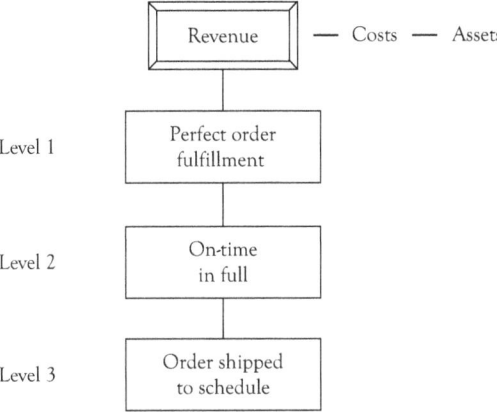

Figure 2.4. SCOR and revenue.

performance indicators chosen is "orders shipped to schedule," an important component of the perfect order.

In addition to identifying the specific SCM measures, companies need to establish goals for each based on the desired level of performance (in this case, 100% performance for on-time, in full and orders shipped to schedule). Goal setting at each of the levels of the SCOR model plays a major role in establishing the level of effort and creativity required to achieve the goal through continuous process improvement initiatives.

Employees in nonmanagerial roles in the organization (say, shop-floor workers involved in producing a product to schedule or the order picker in a distribution center) may not recognize the ultimate impact of their actions on corporate EVA. This situation, common among US companies, needs to be addressed. The objective is to create a true team-oriented environment where everyone from top to bottom understands the linkages in the model. Overall, properly selected and linked performance measures will focus resources on contributing to overall corporate performance.

The Cost Component

Figure 2.5 shows how the SCOR model process can be linked to metrics in support of the cost component of EVA. In the example, The SCOR model identifies "Total Supply Chain Management Costs" as the Level 1 objective with supporting metrics in Levels 2–4. The "Total Supply Chain Management Cost" objective is the sum of the costs of a number of significant functional operations. In this example, only three (supply management costs, acquisition costs, and receiving costs) have been listed. The supply chain manager, who must be familiar with the overall corporate measures of success, should select those areas to focus on that have the most significant impact on that measure.

In the example shown, supply management is used as the Level 2 performance measure because of the significance of the dollars spent on transaction costs (costs associated with the processing of purchase orders) in the supply management process. In some instances, these costs may be as high as $150 per purchase order.

The model focuses management's attention on supply management if one of the objectives is to reduce supply chain management costs. There is great leverage associated with this metric because a dollar saved on transaction costs is an additional dollar contribution to profit-boosting EVA, all else equal.

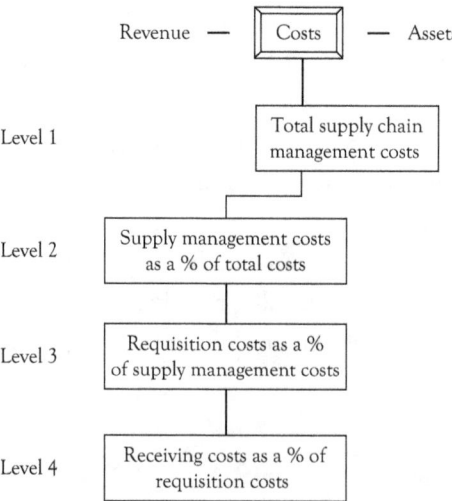

Figure 2.5. SCOR and costs.

The decomposition of Levels 3 and 4 isolates supply management–related activities that are not included in the actual expenditures of goods and services. The example shows product acquisition costs as a Level 3 metric. Those costs include salaries for all those involved in the purchasing process and other transaction costs. For example, one of those costs relates to receiving activities, a component of acquisition costs. This is a Level 4 metric in the model.

Let us assume that a firm buys $1,000,000 in goods and services from suppliers and spends a total of $75,000 on acquisition costs (7.5% of purchases). The firm's research shows that the industry average for those costs is 3.5%, suggesting that significant cost-reduction opportunities exist in this area. Management may decide to begin by focusing on receiving costs because a cost analysis shows that they make up a large portion of overall acquisition costs. There is a link, therefore, between actions taken to reduce costs in receiving at Level 4 and the effort to reduce total supply chain management costs at Level 1.

Peeling away each layer of the supply chain process for every function would produce a very complex network of linked process metrics. That is why it is important to prioritize the opportunities. The goal is to focus on those factors that will most effectively support the improvement in the EVA cost element.

The Asset Component

A number of factors can impact the level of assets a firm employs to deliver value to the market. To have a positive impact on EVA, the firm needs to minimize the asset levels used to deliver that value. Factors such as capital utilization, cash velocity, inventory turns, and cycle time reduction will impact how effectively the firm is managing its assets.

The planning level of the SCOR model focuses on identifying a balance of supply chain resources necessary to meet supply chain requirements. One of the model's key performance attributes is asset level. The goal here is to provide just the right amount of assets to meet requirements. This balance will improve the model's "cash-to-cash cycle time" metric of the model.

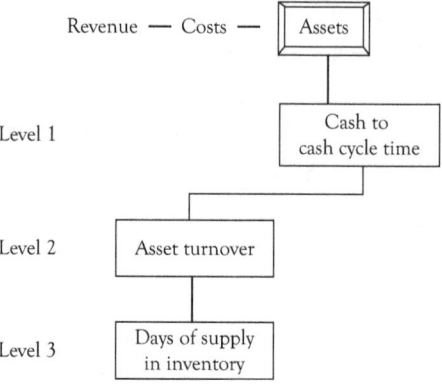

Figure 2.6. SCOR and assets.

Figure 2.6 identifies cash-to-cash cycle time as a Level 1 metric. This metric represents the average number of days that elapse between paying for raw materials from suppliers and receiving payment for the final product from customers.

Cash-to-cash cycle time is, in turn, directly impacted by asset turnover (e.g., raw material inventory) at Level 2, which itself is impacted by the days of supply in inventory at Level 3. Management intent on improving EVA through the asset component can use the cash-to-cash cycle time metric to force attention on asset turnover by setting objectives for days of supply in inventory. A reduction in inventory should increase turnover at a consistent level of sales. Ultimately, these actions are reflected in a reduction in cash-to-cash cycle time. In the end, the asset component of EVA is reduced assuming no increases in overall asset levels. Thus, as with the first two EVA components, the asset component is clearly linked to the overall measure of corporate financial performance.

The benefits of the hierarchical mapping process described for the revenue, cost, and asset components of EVA are significant. The process helps to tie the goals and strategies at the operational level to a measure of overall organizational performance that demonstrates the impact on shareholder value. The SCOR model provides the hierarchical framework. The overall performance measure of EVA provides the link to shareholder value. An attempt was made here to demonstrate the link between the

SCOR model performance attributes and metrics and overall corporate performance.

Return on Invested Capital

Effectively and efficiently managing the value chain will have a positive impact on ROIC. Effectiveness in managing assets and efficiency in managing costs can impact ROIC dramatically. The impact may be substantial because value chain–related decisions will result in significant reductions in operating costs and the level of the firm's total assets. Figure 2.7 demonstrates how better cost controls and asset management will lead to a dramatic improvement in ROIC.

Figure 2.7, typically referred to as the "DuPont Model," assumes that costs and assets are reduced by a modest 5%. The specific impact is on material costs and inventory levels. The result is an increase in operating income from 8% to 10.3%, while the decline in inventory reduces the firm's total asset base leading to an increase in asset turnover from 1.25 to 1.26. (The level of sales is unchanged.) The resulting ROIC (profit margin

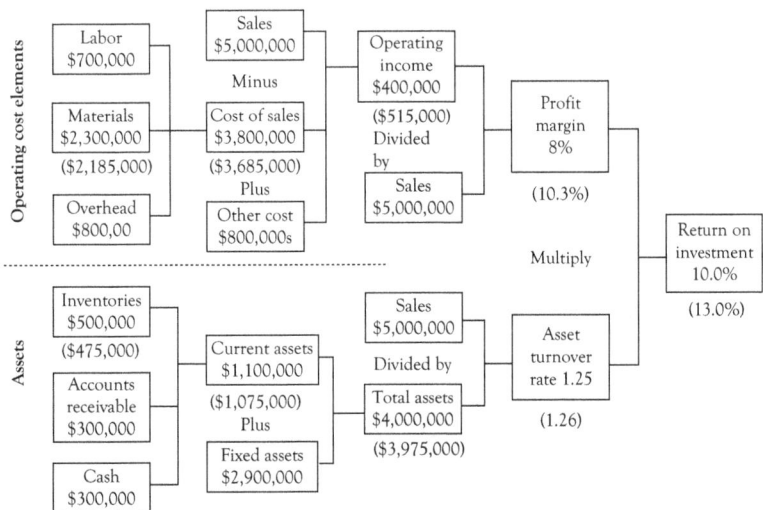

Figure 2.7. The value chain and return on invested capital.

Source: Dobler, Burt, and Starling (2002 World class supply management).
Note: The figures in parentheses reflect a 5% reduction in the cost of materials.

x asset turnover) increases a full 3 percentage points from 10% to 13% or 30%.

Activities in the supply chain component of the value chain—supply management and inventory management in this example—can generate the level of impact demonstrated if they effectively manage the appropriate linkages. Tightening the linkages between the firm and its external suppliers can help reduce material costs. At the same time, close internal linkages between supply management and inventory management can lead to significant cuts in inventory levels, especially if the firm is adopting just-in-time principles. (Note: In some organizations, inventory management is the responsibility of the supply manager. Here we assume it is not.) We also assume tighter linkages among supply, inventory management, and operations because of the synergies among them. Supply and inventory management depend on information from operations to plan for the proper purchasing volume and effective inventory management to assure continuity of operations, all of this, of course, aimed at satisfying customer demands.

A Call to Action

Organizations can take several important steps to help establish the link between the effective management of the supply chain—a critical component of the value chain—and improved financial performance. First, top management must commit to developing an understanding of how supply chain performance can impact financial performance—no matter what financial metrics are used. Supply chain professionals, for their part, can assume a lead role in facilitating that understanding.

Next, everyone responsible for managing supply chain activities must be made aware of the financial performance metrics so that decisions made at the operational level are tied to expected outcomes. Finally—and this important step is often overlooked—a process must be established to educate those in nonmanagement, operational roles on the impact of their daily actions on the firm's overall performance. Using the SCOR model construct to show where each individual's efforts make a contribution can help establish the context for performance. At the same time, it is important to establish a variable component to the compensation structure (e.g., bonuses) based on the firm's overall performance. This serves to reinforce the connection between the actions taken at the daily activity level and overall financial performance. (We take a more in-depth look at this issue in Chapter 5).

Industry leaders today must develop an understanding of how the day-to-day activities of managing the supply chain relate to corporate financial performance. Yet, in all too many instances, that fundamental understanding is lacking. Supply chain managers get so caught up with managing those activities under their control that they fail to make any connection to overall corporate performance.

For this to change, several things need to happen. As noted earlier, top management needs to develop an appreciation of how an effectively managed supply chain contributes to overall financial performance. At the same time, managers involved in the day-to-day supply chain operations need to become conversant with the language of top management. With that capability, they can then put in place a process for demonstrating the significant impact of a well-managed supply chain on overall corporate performance.

Through the use of two important metrics of an organization's financial performance—EVA and ROIC—an attempt has been made to demonstrate the link between the supply chain component of the value chain and financial performance. There is little doubt that effectively and efficiently managed activities in the value chain and the management of the linkages that exist both internally and externally will have a major impact on the financial success of the firm.

Conclusion

This chapter explained the connection between the value chain, its ability to help deliver on the four dimensions of competitiveness, and the resultant impact on profitability. A firm can lower costs to help marketing use price as a competitive weapon to expand market share. It may also charge premium prices in the market if the value chain delivers a value proposition (e.g., speed to market) for which a customer is willing to pay. All of this will have a positive impact on the firm's financial performance as measured by EVA or ROIC.

*A portion of this chapter is based on Presutti, W. D., & Mawhinney, J. R. (2007). The supply chain-finance link. *Supply Chain Management Review*, September 2007. Used with permission.

Suggested Actions

- Design the value chain based on the organization's competitive dimensions. If speed to market is key, then all value chain activities should be designed to deliver on that dimension, and the like.
- Develop an understanding of how supply chain performance—an important component of the value chain—impacts the financial performance of the organization.
- Educate everyone responsible for managing and carrying out value chain activities on the organization's financial performance metrics.

CHAPTER 3

Boundarylessness and the Value Chain

Key Points

- The meaning of the boundaryless organization and its implications for competitiveness
- The limitations of bureaucracy and the bounded mentality
- Typical dysfunctions in a bureaucratic form of organization
- Important keys to minimize dysfunctions to move the value chain closer to a state of boundarylessness

Introduction

The effective and efficient management of the value chain is key to a firm's competitiveness and profitability. Getting there requires that leaders and managers create a boundaryless organization, a fundamental foundation on which value chain management rests and one absent the silo mentality that creates roadblocks to building internal cooperation among functions and external relations with customers and suppliers.

This chapter will define the boundaryless organization, identify symptoms of dysfunctional organizational boundaries, demonstrate the impact of those dysfunctions on value chain management, and recommend an organizational design that may help to overcome the dysfunctions and build a boundaryless value chain.

The Boundaryless Organization

Jack Welch, the former and high-profile chairman of the General Electric Company, is credited with introducing the term "boundaryless" to the lexicon of American business. He saw vertical and horizontal boundaries within a company and the barriers between the company and its customers and suppliers as limiting factors to overall competitive success. The boundaryless organization is not defined by, or limited to, the horizontal, vertical, or external boundaries established in a traditional organizational structure.[1]

The Traditional Organization

The defining characteristics of the traditional organization is embodied in the organizational chart with its boxes containing the typical corporate functions such as accounting, marketing, production, engineering, purchasing, and so forth. This development was a manifestation of Adam Smith's idea of task specialization put forth in his 1776 book, *The Wealth of Nations*.[2] As it turned out, task specialization was a convenient guide to create the organizations necessary to accommodate the explosive growth in capitalist enterprises in the late 19th and early 20th centuries. Organizing by the vast array of specialized knowledge required by the organization to operate made management of those growing enterprises more efficient.

During this period, the writings of sociologist, political scientist, and economist Max Weber addressed the issue of "legitimate authority and bureaucracy," solidifying the belief that bureaucracy was indeed the best form of organization. Weber's idealized bureaucracy contained several features including:

- a continuous organization of official functions bound by rules
- organizing through a clearly defined hierarchy of offices
- offices that have a clearly defined sphere of competence
- offices that possess special knowledge of acts and a store of documents peculiar to themselves
- the ability to make rapid, clear decisions free of the necessity of compromise between different opinions[3]

The first four features create bureaucracy's bounded mentality where each major function rests comfortably inside the boxes on the organizational chart. However, it is the fifth feature that is especially egregious limiting the inclination of those working in various functions to build the boundaryless organization. The notion that those residing inside Weber's boxes can make fast decisions because they are unencumbered of the necessity to compromise or consider others' opinions is a root cause of the dysfunctions in most organizations.

The Dysfunctions of the Bureaucratic Form

While the rules of the bureaucratic form of organization may have been useful in managing the emerging large and dominant businesses of the late 19th and early 20th centuries, they are impediments to managing the value chains in the 21st century. Today, speed and flexibility, two of the generally recognized dimensions of competitiveness presented in Chapter 2, are absolutely essential for success in the global marketplace. Unfortunately, the bureaucratic form allows for neither. Instead, it creates dysfunctions that preclude even a modicum of effectiveness in value chain management, limiting a firm's ability to compete on the dimensions of speed and flexibility.

The dysfunctions are so common that they become a part of the accepted culture in most organizations. Although there may be many ways to describe those dysfunctions, Askenas et al. succinctly captures them as follows:

- slow, sequential cycle times
- protected turf
- suboptimization of organizational goals
- the enemy within syndrome.[4]

It is the rare organization that is not afflicted by one or more of these dysfunctions.

Defining the Dysfunctions

Slow, sequential cycle times is the handoff—a piece of the overall work is done by one function and then passed on to the next function to complete its part of the work, each function sitting comfortably within its box. Each work unit addresses issues it believes relevant to getting its part of the job done without considering the impact of its decisions on the work of the surrounding work units. This dysfunction is the tangible manifestation of Weber's assertion that bureaucracy provides the "ability to make, rapid, clear decisions free of the necessity of compromise between different opinions." Decisions may be made rapidly within a function but if those decisions cause friction with other work units dependent on its work, those "rapid decisions" are of little value in minimizing the cycle time for an entire process.

Protected turf reinforces the functional boundaries causing people to protect the perceived power and prestige of that particular function and to protect the interests of the individuals in that function. People working in a particular function may develop great pride in their expertise and are, in fact, compensated on the accomplishment of individual goals achieved within that function. A challenge by an outsider is rebuffed. If the challenger persists, that very well may create another of the dysfunctions—the enemy within who is to be resisted at all costs.

Turf protection may also create the suboptimization of organizational goals. The focus is working on the goals and objectives that are the priority for a specific function without regard to the impact on the goals and objectives of the overall organization. In a perfect world, the functional goals and objectives ought to align with the organization's goals and objectives but it does not always work out that way. One of the fundamental causes of this dysfunction is built into the organization's compensation system. We discuss that issue in Chapter 5.

The Dysfunctions on Display

To demonstrate how the dysfunctions manifest themselves, let's consider the specification development process in a goods-producing environment. The engineering department needs to develop a specification for a component that will be needed in the production of the company's final product. Ideally, the "good specification" will consider the needs of all of the departments that have a direct interest in the final specification. For example, it should consider, at a minimum, the concerns of the marketing, production, and supply management (purchasing) departments in addition to its own concerns.

Marketing is concerned about delivering a quality product to the customer on time at a profitable price. Production focuses on the ease of use of the component in the manufacturing process, that is, the "ease of manufacturability." Purchasing wants to be able to use the forces of competition in the marketplace to get the component at the lowest cost and to assure its availability to avoid possible supply disruptions. Engineering, of course, is concerned about the component's performance.

The component in question is wiring for a commercial aircraft.[5] The engineering department developed a specification for an industry standard wire but with a ceramic outer coating. After the specification was released for purchase to the supply management department, the responsible buyer saw an immediate problem. The stipulation for a ceramic outer coating converted a standard wire available from multiple sources to a nonstandard wire available from only one source. That source was identified in the specification. The specification as written would not only increase the cost of the wire but would force a single-source situation possibly jeopardizing ready availability and creating supply disruption.

The buyer, a conscientious professional, challenged the specification because established company policy requires that competitive bidding be used when possible and the multiple sourcing (at least two sources) for all critical components. The buyer asked the responsible engineer if the ceramic coating was essential. The engineer was adamant that it was and dismissed the buyer's request that other standard wires without ceramic coating be tested. The buyer, recognizing the potential cost and availability ramifications of the specification, then requested samples of the standard wire without the ceramic coating from five leading wire suppliers. The samples were sent to the production laboratory for testing. All of the samples passed the performance requirements established by the engineering department. The only sample that failed was the ceramic wire from the supplier identified in the specification. It was found to be highly susceptible to abrasion, making it difficult to work with in production. When the buyer sent the production laboratory results to the engineering department, the responsible engineer was unconvinced and refused to change the specification.

So, here we have a series of actions that have seriously slowed down the process cycle time. In essence, a reverse handoff was initiated from the supply management department back to engineering and then back again to the supply management department. Here was the engineering department vigorously protecting its turf. The buyer did not give up. After additional discussion with the engineer, he discovered that the engineering department did not trust the work of the production laboratory, viewing it as illegitimate and an enemy to be on guard against at all times.

This allowed the buyer to try a different strategy. He asked if the engineers would test all of the sample wires themselves and, if the standard wires met the performance requirements, would they then change the specification to make the buying process more effective. The engineers agreed, tested the sample wires, were satisfied with the results, and changed the specification, freeing the buyer to bid the requirement competitively, thus allowing for a more cost-effective buy and increasing availability to assure that stock-out situations did not occur.

Fortunately, in this situation, the buyer used his well-developed level of emotional intelligence to empathize with the engineer's position, to see the issue from the engineer's perspective to get to a more optimal solution. However, it slowed the process and uncovered serious turf protection and enemy-within problems.[6]

If the engineering specification was allowed to stand, it would create the dysfunction of the "suboptimization of organizational goals." The original specification for the ceramic wire was not a "good spec." It created cost and availability issues for supply management because it specified a single source of a nonstandard component. It also created problems for the production department because its susceptibility to abrasion made it difficult to handle. And, it created a problem with marketing because the ceramic-coated wire was heavier than the standard wire contributing unnecessary weight to the airplane. Customers wanted as light an airplane as possible to make it possible to maximize payload (fare-paying passengers). In the end, only the engineering department's performance requirements would have been met at the expense of a more optimal solution across multiple functions.

Minimizing Dysfunctions—A Theoretical Foundation

Minimizing the negative effects of organizational dysfunctions requires the escape from the bounded mentality manifested in the design of the typical organization chart and the bureaucratic form. As we saw in the example of the process of developing the wire specification, this bounded mentality leads to intraorganizational conflict that must be minimized to effectively manage the value chain. Only in what Senge calls the "learning organization" is this escape possible. The key characteristic of the learning organization is systems thinking where the emphasis is on understanding how the individual parts of the organization fit together rather than solely on the individual parts themselves. Leaders in the learning organization help everyone see the big picture and emphasize the importance of understanding how and why the various functions interact.[7]

The importance of this systems, or holistic, thinking is not new. Mary Parker Follett, one of America's greatest management theorists of the early 20th century introduced in Chapter 1, developed ideas like the holistic nature of communities, the importance of reciprocal relationships, win–win solutions, and a focus on process, all of which are key to transcending the bounded mentality of the bureaucratic form.[8]

Follett thought it important to get people to transcend their individual or departmental interests to what is good for the organization. She stressed the importance of seeing the organization as a functional whole for which the participants have joint responsibility. This would work to minimize intraorganizational conflict. She considered several ways through which conflicts may be resolved. They included the voluntary submission of one side to the other, victory of one side over the other (domination), and compromise. She rejected all three, the first two for obvious reasons.

However, it is surprising that she did not see compromise as a solution to resolving conflicts. It is generally accepted that conflicting views are best settled by compromise. Follett's view was that compromise leaves both sides unsatisfied. Agreement may be reached but commitment to the result may not be strong. The key is finding a solution without compromise or domination.

Thus was born her concept of integration, which has come to underlie the rationale for the boundaryless organization. In her words, "Integration involves invention and the clever thing is to recognize it and not let one's thinking stay within the boundaries of two alternatives which are mutually exclusive." In essence, she is advocating using her ideas about reciprocal relationships to pursue the "out of the box" thinking fundamental to getting to win–win solutions that minimize organizational dysfunctions and promote the boundarylessness that effective value chain management requires.

Follett, like Senge, stressed the importance of leadership, that it is important for leaders to view the organization holistically before they can help their subordinates do the same. This holistic view is fundamental to effectively putting into practice the concept of integration. The challenge, then, is how to get there.

Promoting Integration to Minimize Dysfunction

Pursuing integration requires a process view of the organization's work, a perspective also promoted by Follett. Building on her work, many decades later, Ashkenas et al. argued that

> management must view the organization not as a set of functional boxes but as a set of shared resources and competencies that collectively define the organization's range of activities ... arrayed across the horizontal spectrum to create value for customers.[9]

> While the process view will help to loosen rigid horizontal boundaries, it will not, by itself, lead to effective integration. The shared resources and competencies need to be focused on what Senge describes as a "commonality of purpose, a shared vision, and understanding of how to complement one another's efforts."[10]

Senge's observation relates to one of the important characteristics of the learning organization—team learning. And it is through teams, the efforts of which are aligned to a commonality of purpose, that true integration leading to the boundaryless organization is realized.

Turf wars and the enemy-within syndrome—two of the more devastating dysfunctions in organizations—are born of distrust. It is through shared vision and commonality of purpose that allows those who mistrust each other to begin to work together. The shared vision and commonality of purpose create alignment where, as Senge describes it, "a commonality of direction emerges and individuals' energies harmonize."[11]

Too often, teams become dysfunctional because there is no commonality of purpose which causes individual team members to pull in different directions often dictated by the concerns for their specific functions. In that case, alignment is missing and the individual team members are working at cross-purposes. As Senge observes, "The fundamental characteristic of the unaligned team is wasted energy. Individuals may work extraordinarily hard, but their efforts do not translate to team effort."[12]

What, then, becomes the focus of the shared vision, the commonality of purpose that creates team alignment?

Focus on the Customer

In his landmark 1973 book, *Management*, Peter Drucker, perhaps the most renowned management scholar of the 20th century, clearly and succinctly stated the purpose of a business:

> There is only one valid definition of business purpose: to create a customer ... What the customer thinks he is buying, what he considers value, is decisive—it determines what a business is, what it produces, and whether it will prosper.[13]

Ashkenas et al., in their principles for minimizing horizontal dysfunctions, like Drucker, recommend keeping the focus on the customer. They note, "The boundaryless horizontal organization is effective when all employees understand and feel the needs of the customer and all internal processes aim to form and strengthen external customer relationships."[14]

Serving the customer should be the focus for everyone in the organization. This may not be intuitively obvious. Should a buyer in the supply department be concerned with the customer? Should the technician on the production floor be concerned with the customer? Should the picker and packer in a distribution center be concerned with the customer? Isn't it the responsibility of marketing to worry about the customer? The answers are yes, yes, yes, and not solely.

Let's use the wire specification development process example cited earlier. As we saw, four functional departments were involved—marketing, engineering, production, and supply. Each of these departments had its own concerns about the specification—engineering with performance, supply with cost and availability, and production with ease of manufacturability. Marketing's concern was to be able to deliver a finished airplane acceptable to the customer.

As Drucker noted, what the customer considers value is decisive. In Chapter 2, we offered the performance-to-cost ratio as a measure of value. If the company had organized a cross-functional team—one focused on what the customer valued—the efforts of each individual team members would have been aligned to develop a good specification, one that helped to promote customer value. The customer wanted a high-performance airplane that minimized its costs of operation. Therefore, the wire specification had to help the customer get there with a wire that promoted high performance while minimizing costs of acquisition and production.

A very useful yet too often overlooked tool to help focus a team's efforts is value engineering, also commonly known as value analysis or value methodology, developed by Larry Miles at General Electric during World War II. It is defined as "a systematic approach that seeks to improve the value of a project, product, or service by providing the necessary function to meet the required performance at the lowest overall cost." Miles expressed the heart of the concept: "Instead of thinking and talking in terms of things, value analysis changes the thinking process to function."[15]

The value methodology is a team-based, organized approach to improve the value proposition. It allows different perspectives of the team members to be presented in brainstorming sessions that keeps a clear eye on the function that a product must perform and to get it performed at the lowest cost without compromising on quality. As such, it can be an effective way to promote team alignment.

The Starting Point

Trying to achieve cross-functional integration and team alignment for an entire organization may appear to be a daunting challenge. A focus on the customer is the most straightforward and simplest way to get there if management makes sure that everyone in the organization understands what the customer wants and that all processes need to be focused on providing customer value. Starting small can help move the organization forward.

Learning at the team level provides a foundation for organizational learning. It is organizational learning that is a necessary condition for promoting integration. As Senge notes,

> Individuals learn all the time and yet there is not organizational learning. But if teams learn, they become a microcosm for learning throughout the organization ... The team's accomplishment can set the tone and establish a standard for learning together for the larger organization.[16]

Another of the important principles put forth by Ashkenas et al. to help minimize horizontal dysfunction, in addition to keeping the focus on the customer, is to "share learning across (teams) ... To avoid losing critical ideas, information, insights, and competencies, the organization must establish mechanisms by which teams and other groups share best practices and learnings."[17] A fundamental issue, then, is what kinds of mechanisms may be put in place to facilitate this sharing of learning.

We can get some guidance from the work of Rensis Likert, a prominent management scholar of the mid-to-late 20th century who developed what he termed an "integrating principle." A key element of that principle is the "linking pin." In Likert's view, the linking pin is a member of two groups—his or her own and the group one step above in the hierarchy. For example, a production manager has the responsibility for all activities and people related to production. At the same time, he or she serves as a member of the company's management team composed of the managers of the other major functions. In this role, the production manager is expected to represent the production perspective on the management team and share experiences which may benefit other functions and the entire organization. Figure 3.1 provides details of what Likert called "the overlapping group form of organization."[18]

There is, however, a limitation to Likert's linking pin function. It does not recognize horizontal links where one does not depend only on the supervisor for the linking pin role. Nonsupervisory members of one team may, as needs demand, serve as members of other teams. Lessons learned

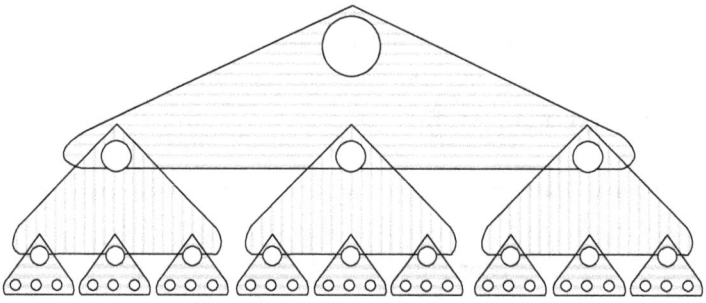

Work groups vary in size as circumstances require although shown here as consisting of four persons.

Figure 3.1. Overlapping form organization with vertical linkages.
Source: Likert (1961).

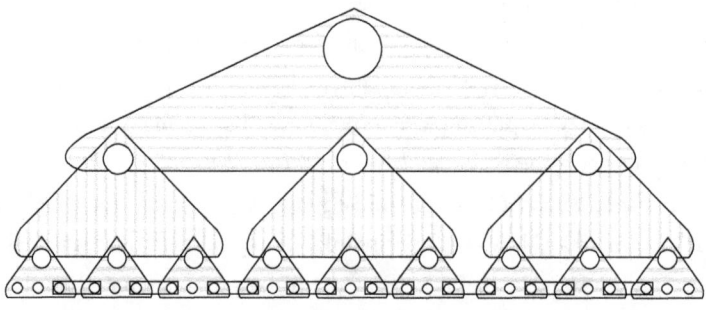

Figure 3.2. Overlapping group form of organization with vertical and horizontal linkages.

from highly functioning teams aligned for a common purpose may then be distributed to other teams throughout the organization. The team members from the highly functioning teams may serve as mentors for other less-aligned teams. See Figure 3.2.

The importance of this experience sharing is a central theme of Nonaka and Takeuchi in their groundbreaking book, *The Knowledge Creating Company*, in which they stress the importance of disseminating an individual's knowledge in order to promote organizational learning. Firms must focus on assuring that newly created knowledge is transferred from a specific team to other teams within the organization. It is important that people share their experiences beyond their specific teams. Thus, a system of tightly linked cross-functional teams is the best mechanism to assure that shared learning takes place throughout the value chain.[19]

Conclusion

Effective value chain management requires a boundaryless organization. The traditional bureaucratic form of organization, with its bounded mentality, leads to several dysfunctions that can be destructive to a firm's competitiveness. Viewing the firm as a learning organization where team learning is emphasized can help create the necessary organization-wide integration fundamental to a boundaryless state where commonality of purpose prevails and the dysfunctions are minimized.

Focusing on the customer as the common purpose for everyone in the organization is straightforward and powerful, significantly reducing the challenge of getting to integration across the entire organization. An effective approach is to start small, at the team level, where members' objectives are aligned by common purpose and knowledge and experience are transferred to other teams to promote shared learning across the value chain. Here the linking pin concept may be especially useful.

Suggested Actions

- Keep everyone focused on the customer.
- Create a learning organization.
- Start small promoting learning at the team level.

CHAPTER 4

Enablers of Effective Value Chain Management

Key Points

- Strategic success requires understanding the benefits of an integrated value chain
- Addressing the enabling factors of enterprise value chain management is essential before addressing the extended value chain
- Leadership direction through strategic plans drives business culture
- The individual members of the organization control the processes and technology—focus on their knowledge, skills, and beliefs
- Affecting the extended value chain can be challenging due to the lack of control/influence, but will provide a competitive advantage
- Trust is a critical common denominator to enterprise value chain and extended value chain success

Introduction

The value chain is not a static entity easily depicted by an organization chart, but rather a living and dynamic business ecosystem that must be nurtured to produce the desired results. As with biological ecosystems, the value chain requires balancing a number of elements to provide reliable results while remaining responsive to the continuous changes in the business and economic environments in which it functions. A great deal of effort is put forth today in developing processes, often enabled by technology, to enhance the value chain. Yet the age-old element of developing the human side of business remains a challenge for many organizations.

In Chapter 3, we defined the boundaryless organization and the dysfunctions that can occur in a traditional organization thwarting effective value chain management. We explained how those dysfunctions may be minimized with a strategy to promote value chain integration within the organization. This chapter will present a more macro view identifying some of the fundamental enablers for effective value chain management. We will assess the enablers by first reviewing the philosophies of Value Chain Management (VCM) and then the role which people, process, and technology play in collaboration to enhance value chain effectiveness. The strategic linkages within and between enterprises must be developed and continuously maintained to meet the demands of the ever-changing marketplace. To address these issues, we will look at the value chain first from the enterprise perspective and then the extended value chain perspective. As we do this, we will discuss the goals and enablers of each perspective and uncover the challenges that must be overcome for successful value chain management.

Value Chains

In Chapter 1, we introduced the Contemporary Value Chain model as the foundation for the overall business philosophy. However, in reality, there are a series of linked value chains supported by a number of business philosophies that comprise the extended value chain. Specifically, while a given enterprise is made up of all the Contemporary Value Chain model elements, it does not function in a vacuum. The common link between these individual value chains is the supply chain, and it is through enhanced supply chain management that extended value chains can be developed. Each echelon, or partner, in a supply chain is part of a network that provides the goods or services to the ultimate customer. Some supply chains are short and uncomplicated, like pick your own strawberries, yet others, such as building an automobile, are extremely long and complex. These complex supply chains have many customer–supplier linkages that must execute properly to bring the product or service to market. To go beyond SCM to extended value chains requires an understanding of the potential value and a significant commitment by the organization's leadership.

A company's Contemporary Value Chain model must then be viewed as an element in a set of value chain models that make up the true competitive value chain as depicted in Figure 4.1. This view of the extended value chain adds complexity to developing strategies for improving and sustaining a functional competitive value chain. Before addressing the issues of the extended value chain, however, let's critique the enterprise value chain goals and enablers, because, if we can manage these well, it will be much easier to address the extended value chain challenges.

Enterprise Value Chain Enablers

To gain true business excellence, an enterprise must develop a strategic focus on value chain development. While each partner in a supply chain is dependent in many ways on the other members of the supply chain, each partner must focus on improving the effectiveness and efficiency of their value chain not only for the good of the company, but for the benefit of the supply chain overall. There may be a few cases of companies that have developed enhanced partner integration without successfully managing the same concepts internally, but it is doubtful that long-term and complex relationships can be maintained.

Before dissecting the enablers of the company's value chain, it is important to identify the existence of differing levels of integration required for value chain success. Not all disciplines or departments in the company need to link and coordinate at the same level of intensity. For example, engineering and marketing for a given product line should be codependent in the same ecosystem sharing collaboration tools, processes, and technologies. However, engineering and marketing for differing products should communicate best practices, complimentary developments, and be supported/encouraged to develop synergistic relationships. The enablers of these two scenarios will differ, and must be consciously considered when developing a value chain strategy.

As organizational assessment matures, many companies are taking a more process-level approach to improvement rather than the traditional

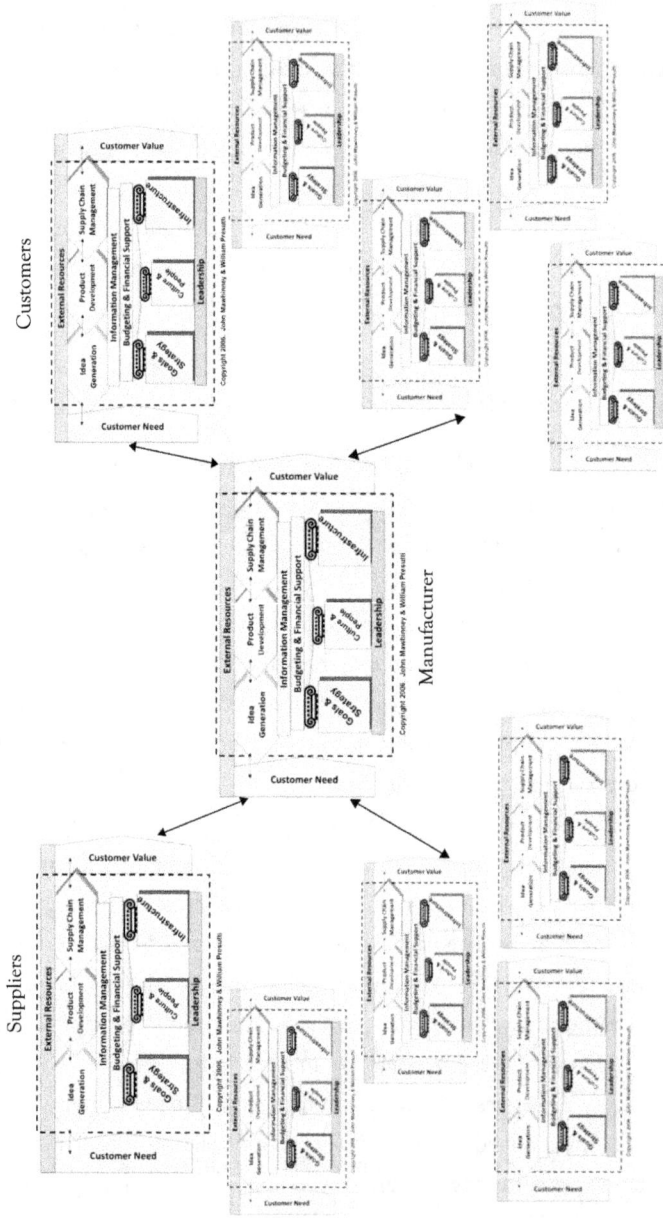

Figure 4.1. The extended value chain.

department view. The integration and common goal setting for segments of operations making up a process is a bit more complex than department-level control, but companies are finding the results worth the effort.[1]

Generally, relationship comparisons are developed for external partners, customers, and suppliers, but the larger and more complex a company's operations, the more helpful the internal comparison of processes will be. The level of granularity for this assessment is dependent on the organization size and complexity. Likewise, the criteria upon which the integration value is determined can vary from which entities exchange the most information, to which information creates the greatest value, to which information is most critical or presents the greatest risk to the success of the enterprise.

In most cases, it is the assessment process that is important as it forces those involved to consider the final outcome before developing the value chain enablers. The Value Chain Group (VCG) provides a well-organized methodology titled Value Chain Business Process Transformation Framework for developing a strategic value chain. VCG has developed a specific technique they call "Value Chain Design" for identifying and enhancing the business process domain and related process relationships. The first step is a strategic value stream mapping to provide the macro-level value chain process linkages (Figure 4.2).[2]

This is followed by a more focused operations alignment with each of the process linkages (Figure 4.3).[3] This two-step process will facilitate an agreement on the level of integration and provide direction for strategic development. With a firm grasp on the value chain integration goal, the current status of internal collaboration can be assessed and the improvement plan developed to achieve the developed goals.

Integrated business planning	Idea to concept	Integrated planning & control	Market to lead
Recruit to retire	Concept to product	Procure to pay	Opportunity to order
Assets & financial governance	Product to launch	Supply chain collaboration	Order to cash
Corporate compliance management	Market to idea	Supplier relationship management	Channel management

Figure 4.2. The value stream.

Source: Value Chain Group.

	Idea to concept	Integrated planning & control	Market to lead
Integrated business planning	Exploration	Demand management	Campaign planning
Product review	Exploitation	Distribution resource planning	Campaign execution
Demand review	Concept simulation & validation	Supply management	Target market sizing
Supply review	Requirements management	Master scheduling	Target market messaging
Financial appraisal	Design engineering	Material planning	Campaign messaging
Integrated reconciliation		Capacity planning	Trade promotion management
Management business review	Concept to product	Product scheduling	
	Manufacturing engineering	Supplier scheduling	Opportunity to order
Recruit to retire	Process calidation	Metric management	Opportunity identification
Recruit employee	Quality/regulatory approval	Production execution	Opportunity planning
Transition employee	Prototype validation		Contract management
Train & develop skills	Product release	Procure to pay	O2O governance
Attrition planning	Product change	Buying channels	
Benefits management		Procurement	Order to cash
Employee lifecycle	Product to launch	Supply payment	Order management
	Catalogue alignment	Strategic sourcing	Order promising
Master data management	Merchandise package design		Order confirmation
Financial transactions	Merchandise package release	Supply chain collaboration	Manage receivables
Item master data	Trading partner alignment	Order logistics	
Bills of material	Lunch readiness review	Forecast collaboration	Channel management
Routing & work centers	Execution launch	Vendor managed inventory	Channel relation management
Inventory transaction		Dynamic replenishment	Channel development
Cycle counting	Enterprise content management		Co branding & positioning
	Product technical information	Supplier relationship management	Master agreement management
		Supplier management	Quota planning
		Supplier quality	Channel performance Mgmt
		Collaborative planning	

Figure 4.3. Process flow.

Source: Value Chain Group.

There is no one formula that will result in a collaborative enterprise that is well coordinated, efficient, and effective in providing goods, services, or both, to the next customer in the supply chain. Rather, it takes a blending of methods, resources, and tools focused on specific goals over an extended period of time to achieve true value chain harmonization. Specifically, these can be segmented into three categories—people, processes, and technology—and the most challenging is people. Processes can be benchmarked, tested, and verified. Likewise, technology can be developed, validated, and repaired. However, while training and educating people can work toward achieving goals, there still exist beliefs, values, and memories that can make change and sustained improvement difficult.

Each business enterprise has a variety of interrelated factors that influence and are influenced by the others. This often complex ecosystem requires the maintenance and care of the organization's leadership in order to optimize the value chain effectiveness. The enablers of this ecosystem are well depicted in Figure 4.4, the Saban and Mawhinney Human Collaboration Model.[4]

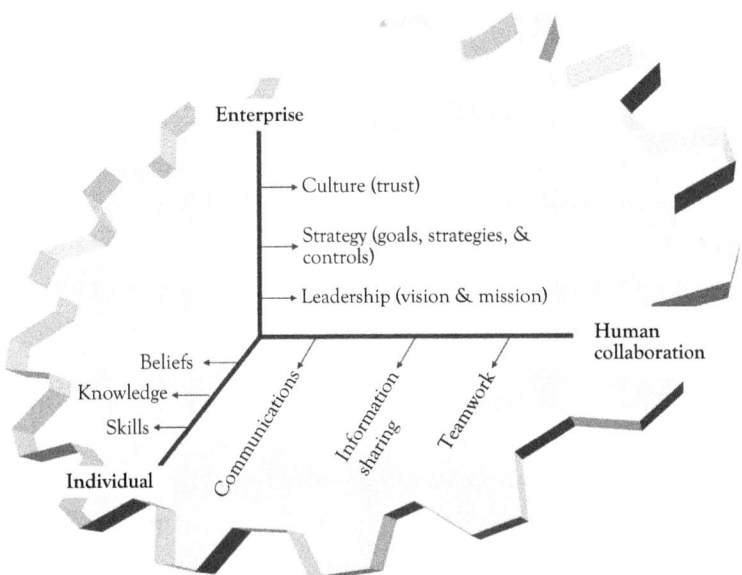

Figure 4.4. Human Collaboration Model.

Source: Ken Saban & John Mawhinney.

Leadership styles are reflected in the vision, mission, goals, and strategies of the organization and play a significant role in establishing the enterprise value chain culture. The individuals that work in that culture will bring their own knowledge, skills, and beliefs to hopefully support the value chain plans. Establishing a value chain–enabled culture is critical to long-term organizational success.

We will build on this model as we review the five enterprise value chain enablers of culture, knowledge/skills/beliefs, trust, change, and processes and technology. These closely interwoven enablers must be part of a sound value chain plan.

Culture

The first set of enterprise value chain enablers is people-focused and is in fact a grouping of interactive and dependent factors. There is much written on the benefit of trust in developing an integrative and collaborative business environment, and the subsequent value generation of such an environment. How can organizations capitalize on the knowledge, skills, and talents of the corporate associates, provide an open and trusting environment in which they can interact, work, and enhance value? Yes, and "they all live happily ever after"; this is not a recommendation for a fairytale approach to business, but rather a case of determining the degree of trust and interaction within an organization required to achieve the goals. Consider it more a factor of environment. Is the business environment conducive to interaction and exchange of ideas and new concepts, or is it restrictive. These values, beliefs, and norms are often referred to as the culture of the business, and a great deal of work and research has gone into developing, changing, and maintaining cultures, but we will focus on the role culture plays in integrating the value chain.

The cultural environment of an organization has many variations from department to department or division to division based on the leadership and management approach of those responsible for the specific group. Yet, there is an overall level of synchronization of organization culture based on the leadership approach of the executives. Generally, business leaders promote and hire team members with styles and values that complement their own or will take the organization in a desired direction.

However, staffing the entire organization this way can prove difficult, so the culture of the enterprise becomes the self-regulating factor.

The continued challenges faced by General Motors (GM) in 2012 as the leadership works on restructuring and revitalizing the business, were evident when CEO Dan Akerson discussed the cultural changes required to progress. The need for elimination of fiefdoms and complex organizational structures, and the empowerment of employees to be proactive and make decisions, he expressed as critical to transitioning the company from the 20th to the 21st century.[5]

The people category certainly includes individuals conducting the day-to-day tasks within an organization; however, in addition, the management and leadership of the company are just as critical to value chain integration. In fact, it can be argued that the leadership and management team are responsible for establishing the value chain collaboration foundation. The corporate leadership sets the direction for the organization through vision, mission, and goals. The subsequent development of strategies and business plans to achieve those goals determine in part the culture and values of the organization. The culture and values will nurture and direct the specific enablers for value chain collaboration.

True assessment of corporate culture's impact on performance is difficult to quantify, but research shows that there are three factors that drive corporate culture effectiveness. First, the setting of goals through formalized strategic plans not only provides direction for the organization, but helps associates confirm the value and appropriateness of their work. The second cultural factor enables communications and coordination of processes through both policy and methods of individual and group interaction. The final factor relates to the well-established culture providing motivation for associates as they believe and trust in the organization.[6]

A study of major Japanese firms confirmed the value of corporate culture as part of organization capital, that is, along with other factors such as customer goodwill, a positive and effective culture adds to the value of an organization. In addition, organizations with strong corporate cultures have an incentive to consciously maintain that culture as it leads to improved current and future organizational performance.[7] As an enabler of value chain integration, a well-planned and nurtured culture is essential to organizational success. What features and values that culture should possess is the responsibility of the organization's leadership.

Leadership and management styles set the direction for corporate culture development. An autocratic and structured management style may provide very specific procedures for interaction and change, but generally provides little flexibility for creativity. In this structure, rules and policy dominate the interchange between people and departments leaving limited need for trust. However, a democratic leadership approach, which often includes cross-functional teams, brainstorming, and open exchange of ideas, is generally less structured and requires more trust by associates in both management and peers. It is in this culture that the associates must perceive themselves as valued members of the organization. As we will discuss in the next section, members of a team bring their knowledge, skills, and beliefs to the group, and if they do not believe they are valued contributors, there is little motivation to excel and continued development is hampered.[8]

Therefore, it is important to understand and manage the cultural factors to support value chain development. Processes and technology can be developed to facilitate the exchanging of information, but creative collaboration requires an open exchange of ideas based on trust of teammates and the leadership. Expecting value chain performance that is based on best practices of collaboration requires a level of trust, and if the environment does not facilitate that level of trust, all members of the organization will be frustrated by the lack of progress and ultimate performance. This example supports the position that the value chain is a business ecosystem in that the leadership and management set the framework for the culture, which directs the level of trust, which in turn sets a level of collaboration that ultimately determines true value chain effectiveness.

Knowledge, Skills, and Beliefs

The individual associate is a critical element in the value chain ecosystem and while people bring many different views and skills to the enterprise, there are some human traits that significantly affect the value chain's productivity. As mentioned earlier, processes can be redesigned, technology can be rebuilt, but there are three aspects of the people element that must be considered when assessing a value chain. These three traits include the individual's knowledge regarding value chain integration and collaboration, the individual's level of training related to the tools and techniques of collaboration, and the individual's beliefs regarding working with others.

Collaboration is part art and part science. People develop various methods of communicating, and in today's society, it frequently involves some type of technology. In addition, each individual comes to the ecosystem with his or her own level of comfort when it comes to communicating with others. Some people relish group success, others avoid conflict, while others lack confidence or social skills to effectively communicate. These methods and levels of comfort certainly play a role in how associates interact; however, most organizations today have expectations related to the science or processes of communication. Despite the individual's method and level of comfort in communicating, it is important that a common body of knowledge exists in the enterprise related to the importance of collaboration to a successful value chain.

Establishing a level of understanding of the benefit of cross-functional teams and departmental synergy is critical for the individual associates of the organization to be contributing members of the value chain ecosystem. Communication alone is not collaborating, yet it is an essential part of the formula for successful collaboration and associates must possess a level of knowledge regarding collaboration concepts and value in order for the value chain to reach its full potential. Many organizations develop this knowledge through formal training in problem solving and decision making, benchmarking, value analysis/value engineering, brainstorming, continuous improvement, and business process reengineering. These methodologies reinforce the need to communicate and collaborate to achieve a synergistic goal that individually few could attain.

While these methodologies raise one's knowledge and understanding regarding the value of collaboration, they also introduce the skills needed to effectively execute collaboration. The specific approaches to improve group dynamics intended to optimize the enterprise value chain results require skills related to data gathering, assessment, and presentation. The formal development of what has become known as personal knowledge management is of critical importance to companies looking to capitalize on the overall knowledge management of the enterprise. These issues are of particular concern to companies looking to better align personnel with new goals and strategies.[9] This need to enhance personal knowledge requires organizational leaders to focus on more than process and technology by developing their own knowledge and skills to bring the "right stuff" to the culture. This includes nurturing emotional intelligence through empathy, forging strong professional relationships, and not shying away from novel challenges, all while seeing the big picture: the vision and mission of the organization.[10]

In addition, today, many organizations are dependent on information systems and technology to enable these processes. We will discuss later the role technology plays in collaboration; this is a good example of how people are the drivers of technology decisions. If associates do not have knowledge of the benefits of collaboration and do not possess the skills to effectively collaborate, having the technology to do these things is of little value. Likewise, the existence of information systems and technology does not enable the desired results unless the associates have the skills necessary to use the tools. These tools range from smart phones, to personal computing tools, to enterprise resource planning (ERP) modules, to decision support systems which are selected by people, management or professional, to enable improved communications and collaboration.

People can be tested on their knowledge and skills of collaboration, and educated or trained to enhance each of these; however, there is one critical factor that is more difficult to assess and enhance, and that is the individual's beliefs related to collaboration. Life experiences, both personal and professional, set the foundation for an individual's beliefs regarding people, processes, and technology. Associates join an organization with a variety of beliefs but of greatest importance to value chain management is their beliefs regarding collaboration and process integration. It has been shown that these beliefs are influenced by leadership and organizational culture. A great example was the New United Motor Manufacturing (NUMMI) joint venture between GM and Toyota. The Toyota collaborative culture could not overcome the GM structured culture to benefit from the integrative lean practices that helped Toyota's growth and success. Only after many years of start and stop successes with just-in-time practices did the members of GM's organization embrace the practice.[11]

One of the most critical collaboration beliefs, whether on the part of the chief executive officer, the manager, or the clerical, is trust. While understanding, training, and knowledge, of collaboration, along with experience play a significant role in how individuals trust the process and technology, it is generally personal experience that sets the level of trust between people. Trust of leadership to do what they promise, trust of other members of the value chain ecosystem to play by the rules, and trust in trading partners outside the enterprise all make up the fabric of trust in the value chain.

Trust

It is true that some individuals are more trusting than others, yet the complexity of the trust element is evident in the many relationships that often exist in the value chain, and the fact that not all will have the same level of trust. The complexity of trust comes from the many dynamic ways individuals develop trust; these include interpersonal, interorganizational, political, societal, peer, subordinate–superior, and organizational trust. From a value chain perspective, once again the corporate culture has a significant impact on the individual's development of many of the trust elements. Corporate leadership values as expressed in vision, mission, and goals supported by resources and rewards are significant factors in determining levels of individual trust.[12] The general human nature of individual trust will result in one associate having strong bonds with some individuals, cautious relations with others, and distrust of others. This is amplified by the multitude of individual relationships required for value chain success and creates a significant challenge and risk. One way business has found over the years to mitigate the risks of lacking trust is the use of well-established rules and procedures.

A "high-trust organization" comprised of trusting associates is much more productive than a rules-based or "low-trust organization" in that trusting individuals or groups are more open to the exchange of new ideas and willing to take risks based on the relationships that exist.[13] Rules and procedures can be effective, but they can also become a crutch to those who are not comfortable in developing business relationships, or are unwilling to change. The challenge to the value chain leader is to develop a culture based on trust and to nurture trusting individuals who thrive in this culture. Getting the right people on the bus includes not only the correct knowledge and skills, but must include an alignment of beliefs, at least when it comes to the trait of trust. Some organizations include psychological testing to assess prospective candidates' willingness to work in teams and to trust others. However, without a trusting culture, those passing the test may soon not be trusting of management or other associates.

To say maintaining a trusting cultural environment, full of trusting individuals, is a difficult task is an understatement. With many potential opportunities to violate trust and create mistrust between members of an organization, there is little chance trust initiatives will not have problems. What is important is that value chain leaders have trust-based initiatives, not programs of the month, but true cultural threads that build a trusting work environment. The greatest way to build trust in culture and individuals of an organization is through example. The leadership and management of the value chain must "walk the talk." Be careful not to initiate any programs (e.g., quality, sustainability, safety, ethics) the leadership and management are not willing to support 100%. For example, shipping defective products to be fixed in the field just to get end-of-the-month billings not only crushes the quality program, but signals all employees that the leaders of the organization cannot be trusted. And, if you cannot be trusted on the quality of product to customers, how can we trust you regarding less important internal things? A trusting culture is a very difficult one to establish, and even more challenging to maintain. It takes a lot of successes to build and one failure to destroy.

Change

The level of individual and cultural trust also has an impact on another enabling element of the value chain; responsiveness. For most organizations, the only thing that is constant is change. Developing an internal value chain ecosystem that can adapt successfully to changes from the customer, the economy, the supplier, and so forth, is essential to long-term sustainability. Most humans do not like change, or at least not significant changes, and one element of managing change is trust.[14] The more the leadership of the organization is believed and trusted, the more willing even the most rigid members of the organization will be to adjust. As a rule, individual acceptance to change fits a normal distribution with a small percentage of an organization open to change, and a small percentage refusing to change, and the majority waiting to decide based on results and their observations, unless the normal distribution has been skewed by a trusting culture stacked with trusting and creative associates.

As with many aspects of developing the enterprise value chain, managing the necessary changes required to guide its evolution toward the corporate goals in an ever-changing environment must be a conscious focus of the leadership. Some adjustments are minor, some affect only parts of the value chain, and others will impact every discipline and associate in the company. The impact of implementing a sales reporting structure change will have an impact often limited to sales, marketing, and customer service, implementing accounting process changes to comply with regulatory changes such as Sarbanes Oxley will have a greater impact, and making the decision to implement an ERP system will often touch everyone in the organization. Therefore, managing change will vary by its reach, but in all cases will be more effective in a trust-based value chain culture.

Enterprise Process and Technology

Many organizational leaders approach enterprise improvement with new processes and technology, and hopefully we have made a solid case for the foundational value of people in the value chain ecosystem. That does not mean that process and technology are of little importance. They are the enablers of the techniques and methods selected by the leadership, management, and associates of a value chain. Therefore, people are the driving force behind selecting and implementing the correct tools to enhance value chain operations. From as broad scope as ERP system modules to implement, if any, to operational tools such as computer aided design (CAD) or warehouse management systems (WMS), to specific decision support tools such as advanced planning and scheduling, the choices must be based on the leadership goals and strategies, and the desired methods to achieve them.[15] The people who make the decisions must have the right knowledge and skills, belief that the goals and strategies are right for the enterprise, and trust that the organization can succeed if the correct infrastructure is provided.

That said, developing or selecting the appropriate processes and technologies is critical to succeeding in today's business environment and essential for a responsive value chain. The operative word in this statement is "appropriate." Once again, the people of the organization drive the processes and technologies; the selection, the implementation, and the maintenance is driven by the knowledge, skills, and beliefs of the people that make up the enterprise. Such changes may need to be supplemented with outside help at times, but the choices must support the goals and strategies, people and culture, and infrastructure that are the pillars of the value chain. Due to the interconnectedness of the value chain, without proper coordination and integration, misplaced processes and technologies can weaken the enterprise value chain. With a systematic design of the infrastructure that is driven by the leadership, management, and associates of the organization, the value chain will be more effective.

This does not imply that processes and systems need to be compromised due to missing knowledge and skills of the associates. New processes and systems often require additional education and training to raise the effectiveness of the organization. It may also require the realignment of talent if the complexity of the processes and technology exceed the abilities of the current work force. A critical support pillar of the value chain is people and culture, and that requires getting the right people "on the bus" and "in the right seat."

Enabling the Extended Value Chain

Now that the enterprise-focused value chain has been enabled, what is required to extend the value chain coordination to include our supply chain partners? If you thought effective management of the enterprise enablers was a challenge, just wait. There are some conditions in the extended value chain that make integration, communication, and collaboration with other players in our supply chain even more difficult.

For starters, they do not work for us, so while good internal leadership will go a long way to directing the organization and strong management techniques can take our company the rest of the way, we have very little control over the value chain operations of our partners. Our supply chain may have bullies, skeptics, or wimps that make it difficult to establish collaborative cultures. Our value chain may be literally geographically "extended" resulting in requirements to collaborate in different geopolitical cultures, languages, currencies, time zones, and so forth. However, while these add to the challenge of an extended value chain, they can most often be overcome and are worth the time and effort to develop a true competitive advantage.

As with the enterprise value chain, the extended value chain strategy must be well managed and focused on making improvements where they will have the greatest impact. Progressive firms are expanding their strategic planning goals to include performance metrics for extended value chain partners.[16] As companies look up and down their supply chain comprised of many suppliers and many customers, the decision regarding where to invest the time and energy for enhancing the value chain is important. However, unlike the internal department relationships, the partner value can be viewed from a couple of different perspectives. One of course is how much business we currently do with the partner, assuming that large suppliers and customers have stood the test of time and as such have developed as a "partner." Conducting Pareto analysis of critical commercial factors such as sales or margin contribution with customers to spend with suppliers can provide visibility of the partner's value.

Another factor involves the long-term potential of the relationship. That is, does the supplier or customer offer a strategic benefit to the extended value chain; if so it would be good to invest in enhancing the relationship. A third perspective considers the value and risk of the business relationship, or more appropriately the value and risk of the products and services purchased or sold to the supply chain partner. Figure 4.5 provides a traditional view of the relationship between the value of items or services purchased and their risk to the organization.[17] Suppliers of low-value and low-risk items that are generically available in the marketplace may not be given the same priority in the extended value chain development as those providing high-value and high-risk items such as

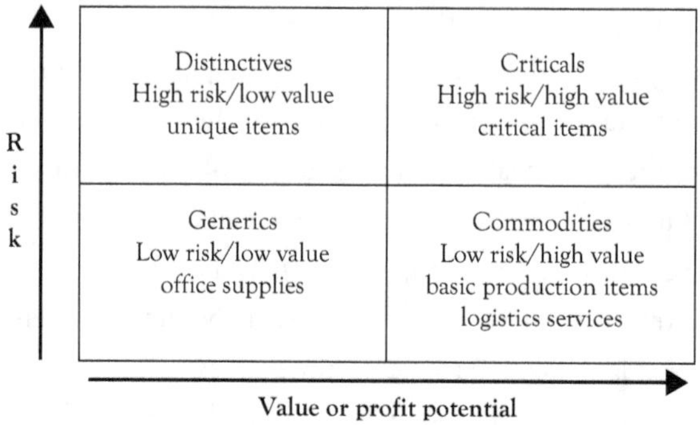

Figure 4.5. Supplier/item importance matrix.

critical sole source uniquely patented components. Given the challenges of enhancing the extended value chain, proper selection of target trading partners is important.

The extended value chain is enabled by the same drivers as the internal value chain. However, the methods required for directing and developing them changes. Let's once again make a quick review of culture, trust, training, education, beliefs, change management, and processes and technology from the broader scale of the extended value chain.

Culture

Developing an extended value chain culture may be more than some organizations are willing to take on, or perhaps more than the organization is able to achieve. However, understanding the existence of an extended value chain culture, and considering it in the tuning of the value chain will provide long-term significant results. There are some examples of effective extended value chain cultures with the supply chains of Japanese auto manufacturers. Although an argument can be made that this is more closely aligned with the Japanese culture, and the corporate culture advantage discussed earlier, the fact remains that there are working models of extended value chain cultures to critique and benchmark.

As with internal value chain culture development, extended cultures require a conscious set of goals and strategies to provide direction and focus. Depending on the size and supply chain influence of our enterprise, support of value chain cultural goals may range from merely being aware of the impact a partner will have on our value chain to actually influencing the supply chain partner's culture. However, unlike hiring and developing associates, selecting and "developing" supply chain partners involve many more factors. How large of a player are we in the supply chain compared to our critical customers and suppliers? How critical are the partners to our business; dollars, risk, or both? How much time and energy can we dedicate to develop the culture; Return on Investment (ROI)? How much influence do our partners have on our business and culture? The extended value chain is comprised of many individual value chains and other members of our extended value chain will have culture goals which they want to meet. Do our goals align?

As every debate has at least two sides, the discussion of extended value chains is no exception. Large companies that often receive accolades for their positive influence on their supply chains may in fact be considered value chain bullies. That is, they really are not collaborating with their partners, rather dictating the terms of doing business in their supply chain. For many having this 800-pound gorilla in their supply chain may in fact be a positive step as they have not as yet consciously taken actions to develop their extended value chain. However, if these requirements conflict with the goals and strategies of an advanced value chain partner, it may result in a tenuous relationship, not a truly extended value chain.

Of course there are other relationship scenarios that may be found including those partners who are eager and willing to work to develop an integrated supply chain and extended value chain. These partners should provide the best opportunity to develop a collaborative relationship. However, there are two other partner types that will challenge value chain extension, the wimps and the skeptics. Companies that have not taken a position on value chain development or do not really care about the processes outside of their organization may well acquiesce to any suggestions for enhanced collaboration with little commitment. On the other hand, the skeptical organization does not believe in either the motives of the supply chain partner, or in the value of extended and collaborative value chains. In both cases, the results can be frustrating and require additional effort to achieve success. It comes down to selecting the partners based on more than just price (purchase or sale) and establishing which will have the greatest impact on our value chain. Can we trust each other enough to truly integrate our extended value chain culture?

Trust

Once again the elusive concept of trust enters the value chain enabler list of important factors, and once again it is directly related to the extended value chain culture we have developed. While developing trust internally can be facilitated with a proper culture based on goals, strategies, values, and face-to-face experience, it often proves more challenging to develop that same level of trust with another organization. Each of our trading partners will have their own set of goals, strategies, and values, which can be assessed, but the people that comprise the organization, and are critical to developing trust, can and will change. Our University Career Services group provides a profile of the average college business school graduate working 5–8 years for five to eight different companies in their career. If this is true, trust at the personal level will require a constant assessment of the decision makers of a partner organization to confirm the level of trust and hence the effectiveness of value chain collaboration.

As with trust at the enterprise level, if it is not possible to truly trust the partner due to being a bully, skeptic, wimp, or other reasons, then rules can be established. Again, rule-based relationships are often effective, but generally will lack the creativity and collaboration of a trust-based relationship. This is not to imply that trust-based relationships do not have contracts in place defining the scope of the relationship. Even Collaborative Planning Forecasting and Replenishment (CPFR), the advanced retail collaboration method, begins with a trading partner agreement. It is merely the case that if personal trust does not exist, results will be dependent on the terms of the contract and will produce little in the way of creative results. Policies, procedures, and technology can enable the exchange of information to improve communications and a level of collaboration, but without trust between the players in the supply chain, results will be limited to the constraints of the rules.

It must also not be forgotten that in the extended value chain, trust assessment goes both ways. That is, our customers and suppliers are working to improve their enterprise value chain enablers and we become part of their extended value chain. As such, we must provide and maintain a level of "market trust" that supports collaboration and value chain efficiency.[18]

Training, Education, and Beliefs

The people development factors, training, education, and beliefs, present another challenge in developing an extended value chain. This is due primarily to the fact that it is very difficult for one trading partner to influence another's selection of personnel or their associate development programs. There are a few methods that have proven successful in enhancing partner personnel selection and development, but these primarily focus on the supply side of the supply chain. As the customer, companies can influence their suppliers through assessment tools such as supplier report cards, which encourage a type and level of behavior that may ultimately require training, education, or new employees. Depending on the culture of each organization and the level of trust between them, supplier evaluation tools can be a driver of creative collaboration or merely the set of rules by which the relationship will continue.

There are some advanced extended value chain developers who have taken more proactive positions with their critical suppliers by implementing supplier development or early supplier involvement (ESI) programs. Supplier development programs range from the customer providing cross-functional team support to initiate programs such as just-in-time or vendor managed inventory. ESI provides the supplier an opportunity to get involved on the front end of new product development or product redesign, and builds on collaborative relationships. In both cases, the customer must see the value and long-term potential of the relationship to make such an investment in the development of the partner organization and its people.[19]

While most of these proactive value chain development programs focus on the suppliers, there are customer side initiatives that have proven very successful. Generally, these occur in the distributor segment of the supply chain and involve training on the product or services being offered by the manufacturer. However, there are examples of companies encouraging fulfillment partners to implement lean practices to improve the effectiveness and efficiency of the extended value chain.

Change Management

As might be expected, change management in the extended value chain may be the most challenging of all the enablers to impact. Once again, our influence in the supply chain, the size of our partners, the risk–value relationship, and so forth. play into the decision to attempt to initiate change in the extended value chain. The most common examples of extended change management involve the rules, carrot, and stick approach. The customer sets the performance requirements, rewards those who achieve those requirements, and punishes (financially) those who do not. Often this is initiated by one of the 800-pound supply chain bullies, but it will produce desired results. This process will drive base-level performance change, not necessarily strategic change.

When an organization has successfully established some level of an extended value chain culture with one or more trading partners, the traditional change management strategies can be applied to the extended value chain. If collaboration is established in a culture based on trust and supported by knowledge, skills, and beliefs true creative value chain management has a chance. Cross-organizational teams chartered to develop solutions that benefit the extended value chain members will find trust-based interorganizational cultural relations a much more productive environment in which to succeed. However, establishing this environment takes time and effort and the decision regarding the critical value chain partners must be strategically made.

Process and Technology

Processes and technologies may in fact be the easiest of the enabling extended value chain factors to implement. This is primarily due to the maturity of many best-practice processes and the flexibility of information systems to communicate and integrate. This does not imply extended value chain process and technology integration will be inexpensive and easy, but the basic requirements for linking each are fairly well defined. The challenge will come when a valued trading partner does not utilize one of our critical processes or technologies. The fact that what is needed to implement such enablers is understood does not mean the partner will be willing or able to initiate such a change.

As critical enablers for organizations and people to collaborate, processes and technologies must support the goals of the users. When goals align and cultures are compatible, the integration of processes and technologies will go more smoothly than when goals and cultures do not align. The controlling factor remains the people who drive the business decision and who must work with the specific processes and technologies.

Conclusion

There are a number of crucial value chain enablers that must be consciously managed by enterprise leadership in order to establish both a strong internal and extended value chain. Most of the enablers focus around people in the organization and the decisions they make. From the leadership's vision and mission, to the skills and beliefs of each associate, the human factors ultimately create the value chain culture, which in turn determines the effectiveness of the value chain. With leadership as the foundation, the pillars of "Goals and Strategies," "People and Culture," and "Infrastructure" provide support for the value chain operations. Processes and technology are heavily woven in the infrastructure and enable the people to execute the strategies to meet the goals.

It is important for organizational leadership to develop a strategic focus on developing and managing the value chain enablers to achieve long-term value chain results. By first creating an effective and efficient internal enterprise value chain ecosystem, organizations will be better prepared to take on the challenge of addressing a well-planned extended value chain. Many enterprises are moving from competing company against company to competing supply chain to supply chain. The next generation of strategic competition will be value chain to value chain.

Suggested Actions

- Keep the value chain enablers as a critical component of strategic plan development.
- Never lose focus of the value of the individual's knowledge, skills, and beliefs in maintaining an effective value chain culture.
- Study the similarities and differences of the internal and external value chain enablers.
- Commit to enterprise value chain mastery before addressing extended value chain integration.
- Create a culture based on trust, internal and external, to experience the benefits of value chain management.

CHAPTER 5

Organization-wide Variable Pay

The Missing Link in Managing the Value Chain

Key Points

- The role of identity economics in establishing organization-wide variable pay
- Integrating identity economics with the expectancy model of motivation
- The chain reaction and reinforcement dynamic of organization-wide variable pay
- The self-financing nature of variable compensation
- Some existing models of variable compensation
- A recommended model based on simplicity, a culture of collaboration, and management commitment

Introduction

Introducing an organization-wide variable compensation system based on overall company performance is one of the key initiatives that should be pursued in the efforts to effectively manage the value chain. Yet, the subject is largely absent in any discussion of value chain–related issues. As we have seen, the value chain involves interdependencies, cooperation, and team performance. Compensation systems need to be designed to reinforce those behaviors to more tightly tie the identity of frontline workers to the goals and objectives of the firm. Organization-wide variable pay for everyone can boost productivity and profitability that generates a return on investment (ROI) that essentially makes the system self-financing. It is the missing link in any meaningful discussion of effective value chain management.

This chapter will introduce key elements of identity theory. The concept of identity economics will be presented with some evidence to show that the American workforce's identity with employers is eroding. Without that identity, the level of collaboration and commitment required for effective value chain management cannot happen.

Effective collaboration will help to define the cultures of successful organizations as we move through the 21st century. It is teamwork and cooperation that will drive competitive success.[1] Therefore, it is imperative that compensation practices evolve to reinforce the importance of those attributes in the value chain.

To this end, firms should introduce a variable pay component for frontline workers as part of the compensation package. A general discussion and justification for a variable component is presented along with an example of how a typical system would look. It is one thing to recommend a radical restructuring of compensation practices in US industry but quite another to put in place a framework to make it happen. Here again the existing literature will be called upon to provide guidance. The problem today is not a dearth of prescriptive literature. Thousands of citations are available that identify the design issues, challenges, benefits, and results of compensation practices to effectuate the more equitable reward sharing associated with successful value chain management, success measured by the firm's competitiveness and profitability.

The literature on managing the value chain is essentially devoid of any discussion on the role of compensation systems. It is hoped that the contribution of this chapter will be to help fill that void.

Identity and Collaboration

How closely value chain participants identify with the goals of the firm will determine their willingness to engage in the collaboration necessary to promote competitive advantage through value chain management. In their work on identity economics, Akerlof and Kranton note, "effective management encourages workers to be insiders who identify with the goals of the firm rather than outsiders" who do not. They note that ethnographic studies show that identification with the firm is important for workers at all levels and conclude that "worker identification may therefore be a major factor, perhaps the dominant factor, in the success or failure of an organization."[2]

In terms of collaboration, each participant in value chain activities assumes a role with the organization with which he or she can identify. Stets and Burke suggest that identity theory puts those roles in an interaction context where the successful functioning of each role depends on its relationship with other roles.[3] Porter's concept of linkages is a tangible manifestation of this element of identity theory. He notes, "Linkages are relationships between the way one value activity is performed and the cost or performance of another."[4]

Does pay play a role? A 1999 study found that firms kept pay high out of concern for workers' capacity to identify with the firm and internalize its objectives.[5] Therefore, there is some evidence that pay helps nonmanagement workers see themselves as insiders committed to the goals and objectives of the firm and that firms may be willing to develop compensation systems to promote that insider view. This position is consistent with Akerlof and Kranton's view in identity economics that a firm would be willing to invest in a worker through added compensation to convert that worker from an outsider to an insider. The key issue focuses on making decisions on how the success of the organization should be shared with all of its members to sustain competitive advantage.[6] There is some evidence to suggest that identity has been eroding. For example, in a 2010 survey, 84% of employees polled indicated that they intend to actively seek a new position, up from 60% in 2009. The poll views these results as a measure of employees' trust in management and commitment to the job.[7]

The objective, of course, is to create a culture where everyone throughout the value chain sees himself or herself as an insider. One of the key ways of creating this insider view is to develop in all of the participants in the value chain a true sense of ownership in the enterprise. In essence, what we need to do is make every person a capitalist. Although the average value chain participant does not invest financial capital in the firm, he or she invests something equally valuable—time and talent. There needs to be a return on that investment over and above a wage or salary if that personal identity with something larger than a wage or salary is to occur.

Since effective value chain management requires collaboration among participants and since this collaboration requires a sense of identity by participants as meaningful members of the team, then reward sharing linking pay to success must become part of the discussion when issues involving managing the value chain are discussed.

Identity Theory and Motivation

As we've seen, Akerlof and Kranton define workers as insiders if they are committed to the goals and objectives of the firm. That commitment will help to facilitate the collaboration required throughout the value chain to attain those goals and objectives. Integrating this view of identity with established motivation theory, specifically the extension of expectancy theory developed by Porter and Lawler, may help to provide additional support for a variable compensation system.[8] Figure 5.1 provides an overview of the Porter–Lawler model.

Essentially, the model suggests that it is performance that leads to satisfaction in the job. Performance, in turn, leads to more intrinsic rewards like self-esteem and feelings of accomplishment and extrinsic rewards, the most important of which is pay. It assumes that if performance in an organization results in equitable and shared rewards, satisfaction on the

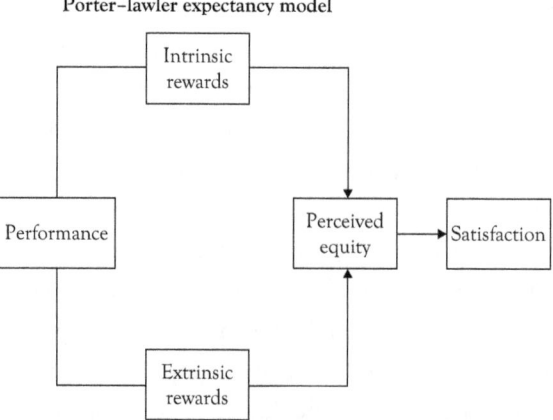

Figure 5.1. *Porter–Lawler Expectancy Model.*

job will increase. It is interesting to note that the focus on equitable and shared rewards is identical to the point made by Akerlof and Kranton as a necessary factor in increasing worker identity.

In that sense, identity may be viewed as an important intrinsic reward leading to more on-the-job satisfaction. For this discussion, the key extrinsic reward is pay and a key to improving perceived equity here is organization-wide variable pay that relates a portion of a worker's pay directly to organizational performance.

However, the worker performance that leads to the rewards-perceived equity-satisfaction outcomes in the Porter–Lawler model does not just happen. It requires, as already noted, "effective management (that) encourages workers to be insiders who identify with the goals of the firm." One of the keys to develop this insider mentality is the opportunity to be involved in decisions that impact organizational performance. As we will see later in this discussion, an involvement system is a critical component of organization-wide variable pay. Involvement in the decisions made closest to the action throughout the value chain is critical to boosting the performance of value chain participants and, in turn, the overall performance of the organization.

It should be noted that the notion of identity may be viewed in two ways as it relates to the Porter–Lawler model. It may be argued that workers as insiders who identify with the goals of the firm will be inclined to perform at a higher level and it is that performance that initiates the chain reaction that the model describes. Or, it may be argued that higher levels of performance are facilitated by an involvement system inherent in any effective organization-wide variable pay plan and it is the increased level of involvement that leads to the intrinsic reward of identifying with a successful organization. As already explained, it is the latter view that is taken here.

The Void in Porter's Value Chain Model

Michael Porter's value chain model was presented in Chapter 1. It included the support activity of human resource management. Unfortunately, his discussion related to that activity is silent on the issue of reward sharing as is the existing literature on the value chain. Here is where the human

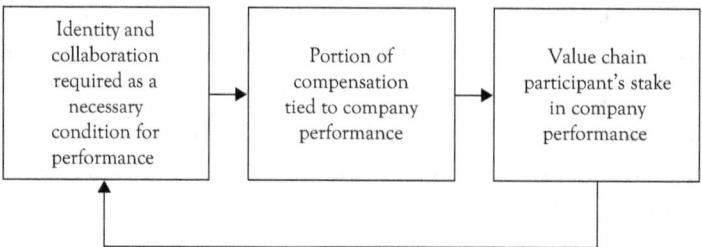

Figure 5.2. The chain reaction and reinforcement.

resource management component of Porter's value chain model needs to play a prominent role. Its role, however, will be dictated by the organization's leadership and the kind of culture that the leadership will ultimately create. As we saw in Chapter 1, Porter's model is silent on the leadership and culture dimensions that are necessary conditions if a firm seeks to change its compensation structure to promote the sharing of organizational success.

The presentation in Chapter 1 of the Contemporary Value Chain includes both the leadership and culture dimensions. It suggests that culture (and the people recruited to work in it) make up one of the foundation pillars of the value chain. The culture is one dominated by collaboration. Compensation systems should be in place to reinforce that cultural value.

A fundamental question, then, is "what compensation strategies should U. S. companies pursue that reinforce the identity and collaboration necessary to effectively manage the value chain?" There is a chain reaction and reinforcement process initiated by the identity and collaboration required for effective value chain performance culminating, through an appropriate compensation structure, in a heightened awareness that the workers have a true ownership stake in company performance (see Figure 5.2).

Sharing Rewards Through Variable Compensation

An expert in compensation systems states, "Variable pay plans are organizational systems for sharing economic benefits of improved productivity, cost reductions, quality, and overall business performance in the form of regular cash bonuses."[9] The cash bonus, paid monthly, quarterly, semiannually or annually is recommended as a key way to help reinforce the behaviors necessary by value chain participants to drive effective value chain performance.

The bonuses may be based on specific productivity formulae, over-all company profitability, a combination thereof, or another system on which agreement may be found.

Whatever approach is taken, variable pay ties a portion of a person's compensation to overall company performance and, thereby, gives the value chain participant a stake in that performance reinforcing the impor-tance of collaboration brought about by a heightened sense of identity with the organization. This approach is much more productive than the continual focus on individual rewards that are typically not closely con-nected to productivity or profitability and what passes for a compensation system in most US companies. Unfortunately, the focus on individual rewards can reinforce the silo thinking and thwart collaboration, both anathema to the effective management of the value chain. Compounding the issue is the near impossibility of closely observing a worker's perfor-mance daily to determine degrees of difference in performance. In addi-tion, it is practically never the case that an individual's performance is based on his or her efforts alone.

If effective collaboration is what is needed to promote the linkages among activities in the value chain, then continuing to focus on indi-vidual rewards becomes counterproductive. If companies are interested in moving beyond the silo thinking that limits value chain effectiveness, then they will need to get beyond the compensation practices of the past and present and work toward a system of compensation that reinforces the importance of collaboration and builds the worker's identity with the organization. Overcoming the inertia to change pay practices may be a challenge but it is a change justifiable by the evidence.

Variable Compensation Pays for Itself

Akerlof and Kranton's model of identity economics suggests that the prof-its of a firm are likely to increase from an investment in worker identity and that the firms are most likely to invest in inculcating identity if it is "cheap." A variable compensation component in a firm's reward structure is a "no cost" way of helping to increase identity. It is the ultimate pay for results system.

Zingheim and Schuster capture the essence of this view:

> The winning solution for implementing a HR program that adds proven value to the bottom line is a variable pay plan *for everyone in the company* (emphasis added). No human resource program compares with variable pay in terms of generating a high performance place to work, creating a culture of performance and getting value to the business through ROI as variable pay. Short-term annual variable pay is justified for everyone in the organization because every employee should influence some key measure of short-term performance.[10]

As for the impact on ROI, they contend that well-designed variable pay programs return four times the cost of the bonuses paid. Even in systems that may not be ideally designed, the ROI is two times what it costs the organization in terms of bonus payouts. In short, bonuses are paid if the company is profitable. If it is not, the bonuses stop or at least vary based on the level of profitability. Therefore, all workers have a stake in working together to promote successful organizational performance.

There is, however, more to the system than the compensation itself. Although much is made of not paying simply for effort, it is important to recognize that processes must be in place for results to occur. Therefore, an organization-wide variable compensation system must be accompanied by an involvement system where everyone can be included in identifying and addressing the barriers that may exist to profitable company performance. For this system to work, there needs to be lots of information sharing throughout the organization that trumps the typical "need to know" mentality that permeates much of corporate America. When one considers the importance of identity and collaboration, the "need to know" mentality is out of step with those important dimensions of effective value chain management.

Consider this experience by one of the authors. On a trip to Japan to visit Japanese companies and academic institutions, a session was scheduled at a midsize company that manufactured night-vision equipment. During the presentation to a group of US visitors by the company executives, the managing director of the facility shared the company's sales, significant cost items, and profitability.

When, during the subsequent question-and-answer session, an American colleague commented that in the United States this information is shared only on a need-to-know basis, our Japanese host was perplexed. How, he asked, do you expect the people working in the company to understand how and what they do impacts company performance if you do not share information with them? And how do you provide the focus for the ideas on improving the company's performance that the management expects? As is the case with many large and midsize Japanese companies, workers are paid semiannual bonuses based on company profitability. They essentially considered all of their employees and managers who are in line to share in the success of the company both through the intrinsic reward of making meaningful contributions to the success of the organization, and the extrinsic reward of sharing of the profits they help create.

This attitude reflects the thinking on what can be done to maximize the chances of success in an organization-wide system of variable compensation. People in the trenches of the value chain need to know how the company measures financial success, the factors driving financial success and, of those factors, which they can most likely impact. Involvement as an element of an organization-wide variable compensation system helps to contribute to the performance levels that lead to a pathway for the equitable distribution of financial rewards as the Porter–Lawler model demonstrates.

Models of Variable Compensation

Companies interested in adopting an organization-wide variable compensation system may draw on a vast literature that addresses design issues, challenges, benefits, and results. On one approach alone, gainsharing, Google identifies nearly 20,000 works that address it conceptually and in significant detail. Common characteristics exist among the different approaches. Successful organizational performance is based, in large measure, on the intellectual involvement by frontline workers in how their jobs are done and a significant bonus payout based on the organization's profitability.

Much has been written about the variable compensation system of the large Japanese companies. First, there is an expectation that frontline workers will contribute productivity-boosting ideas through a well-developed system of quality circles. This expectation is built on the belief that the ideas of many frontline workers are often better than a dictate from management. Company profitability results in bonus payouts paid twice a year, typically in July and December, which may, for the year, average anywhere from 2 to 6 months' pay. For example, the 2010 winter bonus for private-sector workers averaged $8840 (¥718,986 converted to dollars based on prevailing exchange rates).[11]

Experience with organization-wide variable compensation is hardly a Japanese phenomenon. The first significant and lasting American experience with organization-wide variable compensation dates to the 1930s with the introduction of gainsharing. It was conceived and developed by Joseph Scanlon. Scanlon was employed by a troubled steelmaker. He developed a system that promoted worker–management cooperation and increased productivity to help save the company. It was a system through which the company and employees would share in the gains (cost reductions) if productivity was improved. Employee involvement in decision making was also part of the system. Production councils were organized made up of representatives of frontline workers and management to attack production efficiencies and set productivity goals. Bonuses were paid if the goals were exceeded. Seventy-five percent of the bonus pool went to the frontline workers and 25% went to management.

Scanlon became an official of the United Steelworkers Union and continued his work on his gainsharing plan. Early applications of what came to be called "the Scanlon Plan" saw bonuses of as much as 27% over and above the base pay for frontline workers. In the years after Scanlon introduced his plan, companies in various industries had adopted it, "in industries where profits were excellent and non-existent, where relations between management and workers were good and bad, and where productivity was easy or hard to measure."[12] Although Scanlon developed his plan for application in a union environment, it is applicable to any environment and all workers including service-oriented organizations and the public sector.[13]

Several factors point to gainsharing as the most successful approach to introducing organization-wide variable pay to an organization because it offers the largest return on invested payroll with an expected zero net cost to the organization, employee acceptance, no entitlement expectations, and more positive work practices that provide for greater dignity and respect in the workplace. Bonuses are tied directly to improvement in business processes over which frontline workers have some control.[14] Overall, it is not the performance measurement formulae that are the keys to the success of gainsharing. The most critical factors are management commitment, supervisory support and frontline worker involvement.

Gainsharing is not the only approach to organization-wide variable compensation. Lincoln Electric Company offers its Lincoln Incentive Management philosophy that evaluates its employees on work quality, dependability, ideas generated, cooperation, and output. Bonuses are based on an employee's performance evaluation. A formal involvement system is in place and a percentage of profits is set aside in a bonus pool to be distributed among the employees. The bonus payout is significant. Based on 2008 data, the average individual bonus paid to eligible employees was $28,873 representing the 75th consecutive year of bonus payouts.[15] It is interesting to note that cooperation and ideas generated are two critical criteria by which employee performance is evaluated, two of the same criteria important in all organization-wide variable compensation systems.

A Recommendation

Simplicity, a culture of collaboration, and management commitment are key features of the model recommended here. Simplicity requires avoiding arbitrary, convoluted, and difficult-to-understand performance standards on which bonus payouts are to be based. It is critical to success that performance standards be clearly communicated to frontline workers. The lessons learned from gainsharing systems are useful here.

Joint committees of management and nonmanagement staff should work together to establish productivity standards. That approach assures that both constituents have a voice in the final decision on standards. When the standards are exceeded, monthly bonus payouts are generated. This helps to more closely tie performance to reward.

In addition to the monthly payouts, management should commit to setting aside a percentage of annual profits for year-end bonus distributions. This is part of the very successful approach used for decades by the Lincoln Electric Company. The profit set-aside feature complements Lincoln's individual incentive system that may generate bonuses for frontline workers if they exceed productivity targets during the year. As is the case at Lincoln, the set-aside amount must be large enough to make year-end payouts meaningful.

This raises the issue of how the year-end bonuses are to be distributed. Lincoln Electric uses individual performance evaluations which has worked well for them over the years. It takes a great deal of management skill to use the individual performance review constructively. In the view of some experts in the area, few companies possess that kind of skill:

> When it comes to performance reviews, there's no question that nothing is better than something. That's how bad they are ... If teamwork, esprit de corps, and open, trusting, straight talk relationships are your criteria, it's hard to find a single positive that comes out of performance reviews ... Getting rid of the performance review is a big step forward in allowing a boss and the boss's direct reports to communicate candidly about what's needed for better results on the job.[16]

The performance preview is recommended to get to a discussion of expected results. It appears on the surface to be more equitable to provide bigger bonus payouts to those who score higher on performance reviews. This is easier to do if people are doing identical jobs in the same environment. We know that isn't the case in the dynamics of managing the value chain. In addition, trying to make often impossible distinctions in performance to justify various levels of bonuses creates an environment that may stoke competition among value chain participants where internal competition may be disastrous to overall value chain performance. This is where some of the dysfunctions discussed in Chapter 3 emerge, especially the "enemy within syndrome" and "the suboptimization of organizational goals." The solution? "Give everybody the same bonus and you encourage employees to share their competencies rather than cover them over for tactical gain."[17]

As we saw in Chapter 3, sharing competencies is a way to minimize horizontal dysfunctions. Overall, one of the key ways to improve overall performance is for value chain participants to continuously improve productivity that helps the organization compete on the four dimensions of competitiveness—cost, quality, response time to market, and flexibility in meeting the market's changing demands. Both bonuses earned throughout the year and the year-end bonuses help to reinforce the frontline workers' identity with the organization and give them a tangible and significant stake in the success of the business.

Management also needs to demonstrate its commitment to establishing a culture of collaboration. If collaboration among frontline workers is rare, an education program for those workers is in order to assure that they understand their roles in the value chain. In too many cases, workers are hired to fill a specific position without understanding how the position impacts and is impacted by upstream and downstream activities in the value chain, In addition, it is important that the firm pay close attention to hiring decisions to get, as Collins recommends, "the right people on the bus."[18] In this context, it simply means hiring people predisposed to collaboration. Without these efforts, creating an involvement system will have little impact.

The culture of collaboration transcends the horizontal relationships among frontline workers. It also includes the relationships among management and nonmanagement workers. Management must be committed to taking the input from the cross-functional problem-solving teams in the involvement system seriously.

Creating an organization-wide variable compensation system, if properly designed and implemented, will deliver a comprehensive set of intrinsic and extrinsic rewards, including closer worker identity with the goals and objectives of the firm and meaningful bonuses based on company profitability. The leadership of the enterprise needs to be committed to providing

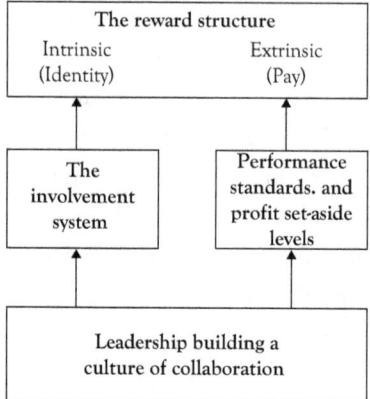

Figure 5.3. A model of organization-wide variable compensation.

those rewards to its frontline workers if it is to serve the best interests of all major stakeholders including its shareholders (see Figure 5.3).

Conclusion

Organization-wide variable pay must be part of the effective management of the value chain. We recommend a model that includes monetary and nonmonetary components that attempts to distill the lessons from practice to provide a simple and straightforward view of such a compensation system. However, the important point is not the specific form that an organization-wide variable compensation system should take. Over the years, much has been written about gainsharing, the Lincoln Electric Incentive System, and other forms of variable compensation. The important point is that it should be done and included more universally in compensation systems as part of a company's efforts to effectively manage its value chain because of the interdependencies, cooperative behavior, and group performance required.[19] Study and discussion of the value chain is incomplete without addressing the issue of organization-wide variable compensation in the value chain and its applicability to all value chain participants.

*This chapter is based on Presutti, W. D. (2011). Organization-wide variable pay: The missing link in managing the value chain. *California Journal of Operations Management 9*(2). Used with permission.

Suggested Actions

- Learn how identity leads to effective collaboration.
- Commit to making "every person a capitalist" throughout the organization.
- Be sure that the compensation system includes both intrinsic and extrinsic components.
- Study existing forms of variable compensation that have proven effective.
- Create a culture of collaboration and build a model of organization—wide variable compensation based on an involvement system, performance standards, and profit set-asides.

Chapter 6

Corporate Social Responsibility and the Value Chain

Key Points

- Corporate social responsibility is a key element in competitive strategic planning
- In addition to shareholder and customer value, strategic plans must consider employee and societal value
- An effective value chain model must assess social and environmental impact
- The symbiotic relationship between the firm and society is driving strategic change
- Society's impact on the firm is evident in consumer and regulatory pressures

Introduction

The idea that corporations should be socially responsible has been around for decades. Chester Barnard, the renowned management scholar and executive at AT&T, addressed it in his landmark book, *The Functions of the Executive* in 1938.[1] At about the same time, J. M. Clark published his work on "The Social Control of Business"[2] followed by Theodore Kreps' "Measurement of the Social Performance of Business."[3] In 1946, *Fortune* magazine polled business executives asking them about their social responsibilities.[4] These early works did little to place the issue of corporate social responsibility on the active agenda of American business.

The modern era of corporate social responsibility began in the 1950s. In the ensuing decades, increasing attention on this issue spawned more empirical research and emphasis on related issues like business ethics.[5] However, it was not until the 2000s when the issue finally gained some staying power. The United Nations Environment Program Financial Initiative released a report in October 2005 which concluded that institutional investors were "not only permitted to but also sometimes required to take such factors related to corporate social responsibility like environmental, social and governance issues into account when making their investment decisions." The report concluded, "Integrating environment, social and governance considerations into an investment analysis so as to more reliably predict financial performance is clearly permissible and is arguably required in all jurisdictions."[6] Thus, investors began to look at a firm's corporate social responsibility performance because that performance impacts its financial performance. A January 2005 survey of investment managers found that 73% of those managers predicted that socially responsible investment indicators will become commonplace in investing within the next 10 years. At the same time, there is some recognition that "adoption of corporate social responsibility policies and reporting are still in its early stages at most corporations."[7]

Given these developments, it is imperative that the issue of corporate social responsibility be addressed in managing the value chain. This chapter will begin by providing succinct and widely recognized definitions of corporate social responsibility and the related concept of sustainability. The focus will then move to how value chain participants contribute to a firm's efforts to become socially responsible through sustainable business practices. We argue that linking the issue of corporate social responsibility with overall corporate strategy is the most productive way through which firms can discharge their social responsibility, an approach recommended by Porter and Kramer.[8]

Finally, we present an argument that builds a case against the whole concept of social responsibility and what we see as flaws in that argument. Overall, we believe that companies need to act in a socially responsible way not only for the good of the society of which they are an inextricable part but in their own self-interest.

Corporate Social Responsibility and Sustainability

Different sources define corporate social responsibility in different ways. We believe this short definition gets to the essence of how we present the value chain and corporate social responsibility in this chapter: "Corporate social responsibility is work that creates value inside and outside of a company by aligning business goals with social and environmental needs."[9] The issue of sustainability is the focus of many corporate social responsibility efforts. The current accepted definition of sustainability is "meeting the needs of the present without compromising the ability of future generations to meet their needs."[10] Thus, integrating the concept of corporate social responsibility into overall corporate strategy is a way for firms to build a sustainable enterprise.

In 2004, Chad Holliday, chairman and chief executive officer of the DuPont Corporation, captured the essence of this view: "We define our direction as sustainable growth—the creation of shareholder and societal wealth while decreasing our environmental footprint along the value chains in which we operate."[11]

Corporate Social Responsibility and Value Creation

Effectively managed, a firm's value chain creates value for both the company and the society of which it is a part, as is evident by the definition of corporate social responsibility presented earlier. This notion of creating shared value is built on the belief that business success and societal welfare are interdependent. This can only happen if a business recognizes the need to address the "triple bottom line" where success is measured by not only economic performance but the impact on society and the environment as well. "In other words, companies should operate in ways that secure long-term economic performance by avoiding short-term behavior that is socially detrimental or environmentally wasteful."[12] Shared value also requires the recognition that society needs successful companies.

Four specific elements of value creation are at work here: shareholder value, employee value, customer value, and societal value. Corporate strategy needs to place the firm on a solid foundation of competitiveness and profitability to serve the economic interest of shareholders. Some evidence exists that companies known for their corporate social responsibility initiatives are more attractive to investors who consider this criterion as an important element in the investment decision. According to a McKinsey study of chief financial officers, the move toward building a more sustainable enterprise increased profits and shareholder value by 12%.[13]

Employee value is created by the types of human resource practices that a company employs. Executives committed to building a sustainable enterprise will, in addition to shareholder value, focus on the human side of the enterprise

> fostering safe, healthy work places and allowing employees to share in the success of the business. Sustainable executives break down the walls and allow knowledge to spread throughout the company, enabling all employees to participate in the success of the business.[14]

This is an important consideration because no organization can pursue a social responsibility agenda with the goal of becoming a sustainable enterprise without the complete commitment of those in the trenches of the value chain.

A recently developed recommended model sustainability policy includes a "respect for people" component that says, in part, "we treat our employees in a respectful, fair, non-exploitive way especially with regard to compensation and benefits, promotion, training, open (and) constructive dialogue with management, and involvement in decision making."[15]

Creating customer value is best judged by the firm's competitive standing in the marketplace. The key question is, "Is the firm providing products and services designed to satisfy customer needs in a way that is not socially harmful or environmentally wasteful?" If the answer to that question is "yes," it will be able to differentiate itself from the competition because it is not just about the specific products and services provided but how they are provided that enable the firm to address its "triple bottom line" responsibilities.

Societal value gets to the critical question of what value (benefits) do companies deliver beyond the specific products and services rendered for sale? This question is sometimes forgotten in the often heated debates about the role of business in our society. Here is a succinct answer to the question:

> A healthy society needs successful companies. No social program can rival the business sector—when it comes to creating the jobs, wealth, and innovation that improve standards of living and social conditions over time. If governments, non-governmental organizations (NGOs) and other participants in civil society weaken the ability of business to operate productively, they may win battles but will lose the war, as corporate and regional competitiveness fades, wages stagnate, jobs disappear, and the wealth that pays taxes and supports nonprofit contributions evaporates.[16]

Business and Society—A Synergistic Relationship

Corporate social responsibility must be integrated with a firm's competitive strategy and activities. It cannot be viewed as a stand-alone effort at philanthropy, for example, to which the firm can point as discharging its responsibility to society. While philanthropic actions are laudable, they do not serve as a basis on which to build corporate social responsibility within the firm's overall strategy. That strategy must include the recognition of mutual dependence:

> Leaders in both business and civil society have focused too much on the friction between them and not enough on the points of intersection. The mutual dependence of corporations and society implies that both business decisions and social policies must follow the principle of shared value. That is, choices must benefit both sides.[17]

Value chain–related decisions made inside the firm will affect the greater community of which it is a part. At the same time, conditions in the greater society will have an impact on value chain activities. Often, those conditions are created by social policies developed and promulgated by civic leaders.

Using a value chain model as a tool to identify the social and environmental impact of a firm's activities can serve as a useful starting point to identify the intersections between business and society. Here the primary and support activities of the Porter Value Chain model can serve as the foundation for such an analysis although we look at most of those activities as components of the supply chain in the Contemporary Value Chain model as discussed in Chapter 1. It is important that management and nonmanagement personnel in each of those activities understand how what they do impacts society and how society impacts their ability to do their jobs. If a firm is to develop a reputation as socially responsible, the actions of all of its members must be focused on that objective.

Let's look at a few concrete examples to illustrate. The examples focus on Porter's primary activity of operations and his support activities of human resource management and procurement.

The Firm's Impact on Society

Let's assume that a firm has built its competitive strategy based on cost and fast response time to the market. That decision will have implications on its operations strategy in the value chain. (Recall from Chapter 1 that Porter's Value Chain model identifies operations as a primary activity. The Contemporary Value Chain model views operations as an important element of the supply chain.) For the firm to deliver on the cost and response time elements of the competitive strategy, its operations strategy is built on lean principles. Lean operations help to cut costs by reducing on-hand inventory, for example. It helps to reduce response time to market because the resulting lean operations maximize production throughput by eliminating unnecessary and redundant processes.

So far, so good. However, a lean operations strategy may also demand a just-in-time procurement strategy to support it. That procurement strategy is characterized by small, frequent shipments from suppliers, increasing the stress on the community's infrastructure and environment. More frequent trips by vehicles in the transportation network will add to traffic congestion and increase emission levels.

The company's operations are positively affected but the impact on society is negative.

The company can develop a socially responsible strategy to deal with these negative externalities. For example, it may work with key suppliers to help with investments in hybrid vehicles to address the emissions problem, or, if the deliveries are made through the company's in-house transportation department, the company may consider investing in its own hybrid vehicles. It may develop a more coordinated inbound logistics protocol that requires developing schedules with several suppliers so that one vehicle can pick up less-than-truckload shipments from the those suppliers and deliver a truckload of supplies to the firm or establish cross-dock operations, sorting and distributing the shipments to multiple locations, thereby reducing both emissions and congestion. Some of the more creative value chain integration initiatives that impact social and environmental factors are evident in the trend toward "horizontal collaboration." Some examples include programs developed between Hershey and Ferrero Group, between Nestle and Ocean Spray, and between Kimberly-Clark and Unilever, which involve shared warehousing, distribution, manufacturing operations, or all of them.[18,19]

Investments in hybrid vehicles or more efficient scheduling protocols help the company meet its internal needs for efficiency that contributes to its competitive strategy while, at the same time, helping to meet its social responsibility for minimizing the impact on the community and the environment. Its corporate social responsibility thus becomes embedded in its overall strategy. This is an example of the observation that "the more closely tied a social issue is to the company's business, the greater the opportunity to leverage the firm's resources and capabilities (to) benefit society."[20]

A firm committed to corporate social responsibility can serve as a catalyst to help spread that commitment through its relationships with its suppliers. For example, the supply management departments in well-managed firms are constantly evaluating the capabilities of potential outside suppliers. They use scorecards in order to rate those suppliers in areas ranging from the quality of their products or services to the capabilities of their management. Today, some firms are adding a corporate social responsibility dimension to the scorecard, rating potential suppliers on their commitment in this area. If the supplier is weak on this dimension of the evaluation, the buying firm can call attention to it and, if the other dimensions of the evaluation are positive, help the supplier shape its own corporate social responsibility agenda. In addition, the buying firm may also look into the commitment to corporate social responsibility of its suppliers' suppliers, further expanding the focus on this issue.

This is important to the buying firm because its ability to pursue its own corporate social responsibility agenda may be helped or hindered by the quality of its suppliers. If the supplier is not committed to that agenda or sees little need to pursue it, the buying company will disqualify the supplier rather than take the risk of doing business with a supplier whose subsequent potential egregious actions may reflect poorly on the buying firm.

On the other hand, the buying firm may be able to use considerable leverage on suppliers because of its attractiveness as a customer to help convince suppliers that pursuing a corporate social responsibility strategy will be good for their businesses. In this situation, the buying company, the suppliers, and the greater society win as the number of firms pursuing an agenda of corporate social responsibility expands.

Although this area of business holds great promise as a vehicle to help expand the concept of corporate social responsibility in the private sector, there is some cause for concern that it has not yet been able to establish deep roots. For example, a survey of Corporate Social Responsibility/Sustainability managers, supply chain managers, and procurement managers indicated that although 70% of the respondents believed that the issue of corporate social responsibility was either "pretty important" or "extremely important" to their companies, just 20% of the respondents indicated that only a minimum corporate social responsibility compliance is a requirement for supplier selection. Worse, less than 9% view a supplier's corporate social responsibility commitment as a critical evaluation factor in the scorecards used to evaluate potential suppliers. Clearly, more work needs to be done if the potential for spreading the concept of corporate social responsibility throughout US industry is to be realized.[21]

Society's Impact on the Firm

A firm does not operate in a vacuum. It depends on society to pursue its competitive strategy. Therefore, it needs a healthy society to succeed. Factors like the quality of education, health care, and good government (e.g., fair and effective regulation that protects both the consumers and businesses) are essential ingredients to the success of the firm. Let's use education quality as an example.

A well-educated workforce is the most critical resource in order for firms to compete in the 21st-century global economy. Therefore, they need to depend on society's education system to provide a competent workforce on which to draw. This is another area that clearly demonstrates the interdependence between business and society. Here is an example based on one of the author's experience in Japan.

Toyota operates its production facilities using the principles of the Toyota Production System or what is more commonly called just-in-time production with total quality control. An important component of that system is the contributions of frontline workers. They are expected to understand the details of the system and the tools of analysis that are required to keep the system operating at peak levels. The tools of analysis are used to expose problems with the system to facilitate immediate remediation. They include quality dispersion charts, defect frequency rates and trends, statistical process control charts, and cause-and-effect diagrams (Ishikawa diagrams).[22] Therefore, Toyota requires a workforce that understands those tools and is comfortable working with them. Many of the tools require a deftness in statistical analysis.

In order to ensure a steady supply of qualified workers, one of Toyota's human resource strategies is to fund a high school near its "Toyota City" complex in Nagoya, Japan. Part of the school's mission is to prepare students who may not be going on to higher education to work in Toyota's facilities and to be able to "hit the ground running" after graduation. Toyota used the existing school infrastructure as a target of its investment to provide itself the requisite supply of qualified workers. The benefit to society was an educated and employable workforce in good jobs immediately after high-school graduation. Thus, the discharge of part of Toyota's corporate social responsibility was embedded in its human resource strategy.

Microsoft Corporation provides another example of the interrelationship between a firm and the greater society. The education system was not producing enough information technology workers to help support the company's growth. Therefore, the company invested $50 million over a 5-year period in the nation's community colleges to help with curriculum development, technology updates, and faculty development. This initiative had a significant benefit on the communities in which Microsoft invested while, at the same time, addressing a critical human resource need.[23]

Overall, a company must be cognizant of the resources in the society of which it is a part—resources that may provide support for the company's strategy or the shortcomings in the society that may put limits on the implementation of its strategy. In the latter case, developing a strategy that benefits the company and society is the best way to satisfy the company's responsibility to the greater society.

These examples demonstrate the key to a company's approach in carrying out its responsibilities to society and what society can expect from the private sector. The following observation captures the essence of this view:

> No business can solve all of society's problems or bear the cost of doing so. Instead, each company must select issues that intersect with its particular business interest . . . The essential test that should guide corporate social responsibility is not whether a cause is worthy but whether it presents an opportunity to create shared value—that is, a meaningful benefit for society that is also valuable to the business.[24]

The Role of the Reverse Value Chain

For centuries, the primary focus on industry and commerce was to deliver goods and services to satisfy customer needs. However, a series of customer and regulatory changes over the past few decades has added a whole new dimension to supply chain management, and the effective management of this value chain segment is often referred to as Reverse Logistics (RL). The increased demand for greater variety of goods from a much more discriminating buyer has led to a significant growth in returns of products for a variety of reasons from poor quality, to not meeting expectations, to "I made a mistake." Consumer and commercial buyers have raised the bar in terms of the supplier's responsibility for their product's quality and performance while reducing their tolerance for deviations from desired needs.

At the same time, consumers and some governments have begun to hold manufacturers responsible for the life cycle of their products. What happens to the appliance or automobile when it has lived its useful life, what happens to all the packaging used to ensure brand identification and safe product delivery, and what happens to unwanted products, whether sold or still on the shelf? The aggressive recycling regulations of the European Union (EU) are having far-reaching effects as companies in other parts of the world compete for EU customers, or EU companies set up operations in other regions. The EU Waste Electrical and Electronic Equipment (WEEE) directive is a prime example of governmental requirements on manufacturers to take responsibility for the life cycle of the product and ensure proper recycling. The directive requires manufacturers or distributors of electronic and electrical equipment sold in the EU to establish a process for collection and proper disposal of the items they make, sell, or perform both.[25]

These changes require the value chain leaders to adapt strategies and infrastructure to comply with the new market or government demands. While the nature of the items being managed in the reverse logistics operations varies considerably from good product to recycled material, the need to capture the potential value and minimize the impact on traditional outbound operations is critical. Forecasting not only what customers will buy, but what they will return is critical to maintaining value chain balance. Allocation of resources, accounting for good product returning to inventory, and capturing potential value from returned items may place an added burden on the organization, but it also provides an opportunity to reap financial gains while being socially responsible. The historic trends and sustainability indicators point to a continued growth in the need for a well-developed and managed reverse value chain.

The Case Against Corporate Social Responsibility

There are those who argue that in the course of managing its value chain, a firm should not be encumbered by worrying about its social responsibility. This point of view is captured in the following observation:

> In cases where private profits and public interests are aligned, the idea of corporate social responsibility is irrelevant. Companies that simply do everything they can to boost profits will end up increasing social welfare. In circumstances in which profits and social welfare are in direct opposition, an appeal to corporate social responsibility will almost always be ineffective, because executives are unlikely to act voluntarily in the public interest and against shareholder interests . . . . The fact is that while companies sometimes can do well by doing good, more often they can't. Because in most cases, doing what's best for society means sacrificing profits.[26]

This view is consistent with those of the late economist Milton Friedman and others who argued that a corporation's purpose is to maximize return to shareholders, and that since only people can have social responsibilities, corporations are only responsible to their shareholders and not to society as a whole.[27]

We believe there are some serious flaws in this viewpoint. First, can we assume that when companies do everything they can to boost profits that society will benefit? Recent examples suggest not, including the British Petroleum's (BP) oil spill in the Gulf of Mexico and the near meltdown of the financial markets because of some unscrupulous profit-boosting business practices on Wall Street. Can one ever forget the experience of the Ford Pinto when the Ford Motor Company made a conscious decision not to recall the vehicle because of a faulty fuel tank that exploded due to rear-end collisions? The company's decision was based on a profit calculation alone—that it would cost more to recall the vehicles for repair than paying claims to those injured or killed as a result of the faulty fuel tanks.

Does doing what's best for society mean sacrificing profits? If, as part of its competitive strategy, a firm needs to find ways to relentlessly attack its costs, it may do so in a way that will also have benefits to society. For example, if the firm decides to replace its gas-guzzling truck fleet with a fleet of hybrid vehicles, it will most likely significantly reduce its operating expenses while benefiting the environment. Both the business and society win. As we noted earlier, the argument has been made that a firm cannot address all of society's issues. However, if it focuses on those issues that directly relate to its business, it can create shared value, the real test of a sound social responsibility strategy. As society's awareness of the issue of corporate social responsibility grows, "adding a social dimension to the value proposition offers a new frontier in competitive positioning."[28] Therefore, social responsibility considerations need to be an important component in the management of the value chain.

Corporate Social Responsibility's Time has Come

As we have discussed, the ways in which an organization takes responsibility for the social and environmental factors within their control varies, as do the drivers. In some third-world countries, little attention is given by resident organizations to social and environmental welfare. In the EU, some aspects of social responsibility are regulated. Some industries have strong nongovernment organizations (NGOs) bringing social pressure for social responsibility, environmental responsibility, or both. Whatever the driver, many organizations are stepping up their strategic focus to take on social responsibility.

The challenge for most organizations becomes establishing the scope and magnitude of the social responsibility reach. With a number of elements involved, that is, labor, GHG, community, and so forth, how does a company effectively establish legitimate strategies to address these issues? Fortunately, a great deal of work has been done by organizations focused on social and environmental sustainability. The following examples provide insights into the direction and magnitude of this work, but are by no means an exhaustive listing of the guidance available to those working on developing stronger socially responsible value chains.

Environmental

In the mid-1990s, two organizations, the World Resource Institute (WRI) and World Business Council for Sustainable Development (WBCSD), began a collaborative effort to establish standards for companies to measure, report, and reduce greenhouse gas (GHG) emissions. Their efforts resulted in four sets of guidelines that are part of the GHG Protocol. The guidelines provide a map for those organizations seeking to improve social responsibility to apply common techniques and metrics to the monitoring and reporting of GHGs. The four standards are:

- Corporate Accounting and Reporting Standards (Corporate Standard)
- Project Accounting Protocol and Guidelines
- Corporate Value Chain (Scope 3) Accounting and Reporting Standard
- Product Life Cycle Accounting and Reporting Standard

While the titles of the standards explain the scope, each was developed in response to differing environmental improvement needs expressed by companies, government agencies, NGOs, the public, and so forth. The value of these standards and guidelines is evident in the extensive adoption by companies and countries around the world. With 138 corporate and government agencies from 21 countries utilizing the GHG Protocol standards, the adoption rate continues to grow in response to corporate recognition of the importance of environmental responsibility.

For example, GHG Protocol teams have identified three levels or "scopes" of emission's to be monitored and managed. Scope 1 emissions include those under direct control of the organization, Scope 2 emissions are associated with the power a company uses, and Scope 3 emissions are those of the other members of the extended value chain that are directly associated with the products or services source and deliver segments of the supply chain. Many companies have begun work on Scope 1 and 2 as these are the easiest to measure and control; however, the trend to tighter control of Scope 3 emissions is gaining momentum, especially in Europe.

The value and acceptance of the GHG Protocol standards were confirmed in 2006, when the International Organization for Standardization (ISO) adopted the Corporate Accounting and Reporting Standards as the structure for ISO 14064-I (Specification with Guidance at the Organization Level for Quantification and Reporting of Greenhouse Gas Emissions and Removals).[29] With ISO 14064 as a global guideline, standardization is continuing to solidify, making the establishment of corporate GHG goals less risky and more widely recognized.

Social Responsibility

In 2001, the ISO Committee on Consumer Policy identified the need for corporate guidance related to social responsibility. Over the next 9 years, work progressed to the introduction of ISO 26000, Guidance on Social Responsibility. While not a certification, the guidelines provide a comprehensive set of recommendations focused on seven areas for organizational social responsibility development. These areas include: the organization, human rights, labor practices, the environment, fair operating practices, consumer issues, and community involvement and development. The guidelines provide a comprehensive approach to addressing social responsibility issues from an impressive and diverse development group consisting of representatives from manufacturing industries, government, labor, consumers, NGOs, service industries, and research. The 450 developers and 210 observers hailed from 99 ISO member countries and 42 liaison organizations, leading to the importance and credibility of the guidelines.[30]

Conclusion

A firm can meet its corporate social responsibilities through the effective management of the value chain. The way the activities in the value chain are managed will impact the greater society, while societal factors impact the performance of those activities. This effort must be guided by the concept of shared value, that there exists a mutuality of benefits to the firm and the greater society of which it is a part.

An individual firm cannot address all of society's issues. Therefore, it should focus on those that intersect most closely with its business. In that way, its corporate social responsibility strategy may become part of the more general corporate strategy. This approach gives social responsibility staying power because the company can address it as part of the normal course of managing its value chain. This is preferable over more disjointed efforts like random acts of philanthropy. One must view a firm's efforts at achieving the triple bottom line (economic, social, and environmental) not as a tradeoff between profits and social responsibility but as a way to benefit both the firm and society. Corporate social responsibility, effectively discharged through value chain activities, and profits that provide an acceptable return to investors are not mutually exclusive.

The future of social responsibility appears to be one of continued interest and growth. William McDonough and Dr Michael Braungart have brought the research from their 1992 work, "The Hannover Principles: Design for Sustainability," and their 2002 work, "Cradle to Cradle: Remaking the Way We Make Things," to maturity in the Cradle to Cradle Product Innovations Institute. Product certification by the institute requires management of the product life cycle from design to reuse by rating products in five categories: renewable energy, clean water, material health, social responsibility, and material reutilization. This 2010 initiative has certified almost 400 products from 90 different manufacturers and continues to grow.[31] Cradle to Cradle is just one example of the trend toward a more socially responsible set of global value chains.

Suggested Actions

- Broaden strategic planning to encompass specific employee and societal values.
- Seek the social and environmental improvements that can contribute to corporate competitiveness.
- Commit to remain current on social and environmental regulations and guidelines.
- Create a culture of corporate social responsibility that extends to your value chain partners.

Notes

Chapter 1

1. Porter (1985).
2. Porter (1985), p. 48.
3. Porter (1985), p. 41.
4. Nelson, Moody, and Stegner (2001), p. 7.
5. Bossidy and Charan (2002).
6. Follett (1933), pp. 47–60.
7. Senge (1990), p. 353.
8. Mintzberg (2006).
9. Boundarylessness is a term introduced by Jack Welch, former CEO of General Electric Corporation, in describing an important characteristic of a successful company where the walls between organizational functions, customers, and suppliers are eliminated.
10. Pascale and Athos (1981), p. 202.
11. Collins (2001).
12. Kerr (1975).
13. Bal and Teo (2000).
14. Bennis (1993).
15. Chandler (1962).
16. Porter (1985).
17. Friedman (2006).
18. Ashkenas et al. (1995).
19. Value engineering is a concept developed in the 1940s by Larry Miles at General Electric Corporation. It looks at the function–cost relationship. The key is to find a product that will deliver the intended function at the lowest overall cost while not compromising on quality.
20. EVA is a comprehensive measure of a firm's financial performance developed by Stern Stewart Co. It considers net profit after taxes less the cost of capital to determine the extent to which the firm earns a return greater than the cost of capital. Key components of EVA are revenues, costs, and assets.
21. Monczka, Trent, and Handfield (2005), p. 9.
22. The "source-make-deliver" sequence demonstrated in Figure 1.7 is adopted from the Supply Chain Operations Reference (SCOR) Model of the Supply Chain Council.
23. Friedman (2006).

24. The Aberdeen Group (2001).
25. The triple bottom line refers to the impact of a firm's activities not only on profit but also on society and the environment.
26. A common definition of reverse logistics is the process of planning, implementing, and controlling the efficient, cost-effective flow of materials, in-process inventory, finished goods, and related information from the point of consumption to the point of origin for the purpose of recapturing value or proper disposal.
27. Collins (2001).
28. Porter (1985), p. 43.
29. Drucker (1973), p. 79.
30. Drucker (1973), p. 60.
31. Drucker (1973), p. 80.

Chapter 2

1. Friedman (2006).
2. Porter (1985), pp. 11–16.
3. Porter (1985), p. 18.
4. Porter (1985), p. 53.
5. The Supply Chain Council (2007).
6. For more on EVA, see Stern-Stewart website at www.sternstewart.com
7. Vickery, Jayaram, Droge, and Catalone (2003).
8. Colman (2003).
9. Kaplan and Norton (1996).
10. Prober (2000).
11. Aberdeen Group (2001).

Chapter 3

1. Wikipedia (2012).
2. Smith (1776).
3. Weber (1947 translation).
4. Ashkenas et al. (1995).
5. This example is based on a case study, Dynamic Aircraft, by Dobler, Lee, and Burt (1995) in *Purchasing and Supply Management: Text and Cases*.
6. Goleman (1995).
7. Senge (1990).
8. Follett (1933).
9. Ashkenas et al. (1995).

10. Senge (1990).
11. Senge (1990).
12. Senge (1990).
13. Drucker (1973).
14. Ashkenas et al. (1995).
15. Lawrence D. Miles Foundation (2012).
16. Senge (1990).
17. Ashkenas et al. (1995).
18. Likert (1961).
19. Nonaka and Takeuchi (1995).

Chapter 4

1. Bowersox, Closs, and Cooper (2002).
2. www.value-chain.org/bptf/ValueChainDesign/ (retrieved July 7, 2012).
3. www.value-chain.org/bptf/ValueChainDesign/ (retrieved July 7, 2012).
4. Saban and Mawhinney (2010).
5. Krisher (2012).
6. Hirota (2010).
7. Hirota, Kubo, and Miyajima (2007).
8. Blair (2012).
9. Agnihotri and Troutt (2009).
10. Friedman (2006).
11. Narasimhan, Kull, and Nahm (2012).
12. Joseph and Winston (2005).
13. Covey and Merrill (2006).
14. Matejka (1991).
15. Ross (2011).
16. Coyle, Langley, Gibson, Novack, and Bardi (2013).
17. Coyle, Langley, Gibson, Novack, and Bardi (2013).
18. Covey and Merrill (2006).
19. Monczka, Handfield, Giunipero, and Patterson (2011).

Chapter 5

1. Goleman (1995).
2. Akerlof and Kranton (2010), p. 59.
3. Stets and Burke (2000).
4. Porter (1985), p. 48.
5. Bewley (1999).

6. Akerlof and Kranton (2010).
7. www. Jobfunctions.bnet.com (retrieved April 1, 2011).
8. Porter and Lawler (1968).
9. Schuster (2007).
10. Zingheim and Schuster (2007).
11. Guze (2011).
12. Time (1955).
13. Mericle and Kim (2004).
14. Hill (2000).
15. PRNewswire-first call (retrieved June 13, 2011).
16. Cuthbert (2010), pp. 2–11.
17. Cuthbert (2010), p. 218.
18. Collins (2001).
19. Mericle and Kim (2004).

Chapter 6

1. Barnard (1938).
2. Clark (1939).
3. Kreps (1940).
4. Bowen (1953).
5. Carroll, Archie (1999).
6. www.asyousow.org (retrieved August 2, 2012).
7. www.asyousow.org
8. Porter and Kramer (2006).
9. www.businessearth.com (retrieved July 30, 2012).
10. www.asyousow.org
11. Jackson and Nelson (2004).
12. Porter and Kramer (2006).
13. Byrne (2010).
14. Byrne (2010).
15. Blackburn (2008).
16. Porter and Kramer (2006).
17. Porter and Kramer (2006).
18. Slegfried (2012).
19. Cooke (2011).
20. Porter and Kramer (2006).
21. Gordon and Levin (2009).
22. Schonberger (1982).
23. Porter and Kramer (2006).
24. Porter and Kramer (2006).

25. ec.europa.eu/environment/waste/weee/index_en.htm (retrieved August 9, 2012).

26. Karnani (2010).

27. www.wikipedia.org (retrieved August 2, 2012).

28. Porter and Kramer (2006).

29. www.ghgprotocol.org (retrieved August 12, 2012).

30. www.iso.org/iso/home/standards/iso26000 (retrieved August 17, 2012).

31. www.c2ccertified.org/ (retrieved August 27, 2012).

References

Aberdeen Group (2001). *E-sourcing: Negotiating value in a volatile economy—An executive white paper*. Boston, MA: Aberdeen Group.

Agnihotri, R., & Trout, M. (2009). The effective use of technology in personal knowledge management: A framework of skills, tools, and user context. *Online Information Review 33*(2), 329–342.

Akerlof, G. A., & Kranton, R. (2010). *Identity economics*. Princeton, NJ: Princeton University Press.

Ashkenas et al. (1995). *The boundaryless organization*. San Francisco, CA: Jossey-Bass.

Bal, J., & Teo, P. K. (2000). Implementing virtual teamworking. *Logistics Information Management 13*(6), 346–352.

Barnard, Chester I. (1938). *The Functions of the executive*. Cambridge, MA: Harvard University Press.

Bennis, W. (1993). *An invented life: Reflections on leadership and change*. Reading, MA: Addison-Wesley.

Bewley, Truman (1999). *Why wages don't fall during a recession*. Cambridge, MA: Harvard University Press.

Blackburn, W. R. (2008). *The sustainability handbook*. Washington, DC: Environmental Law Institute.

Blair, B. (2012). Inspire passion through value. *Inside Supply Management*, March.

Bossidy, L., & Charan, R. (2002). *Execution*. New York, NY: Crown Business.

Bowersox, D., Closs, D., & Cooper, M. B. (2002). *Supply chain logistics management*. Boston, MA: McGraw-Hill Irwin.

Byrne, J. (2010). The sustainable executive creates a bridge to the future. *Pittsburgh, Post-Gazette*, March 16.

Carroll, Archie B. (1999). Corporate social responsibility: Evolution of a definitional construct. *Business and Society 38*(3), September, pp. 268–295.

Clark J. M. (1939). *Social control of business*. New York: McGraw-Hill.

Chandler, A. (1962). *Strategy and structure*. Boston, MA: MIT Press.

Collins, J. (2001). *Good to great*. New York: Harper Business.

Colman, Robert (2003). Effective supply chain management boosts profits. *CMA Management*, December/January.

Cooke, J. (2011). Sharing supply chains for mutual gain. *Supply Chain Quarterly*, Quarter 2, pp. 38–41.

Corporate Social Responsibility. Retrieved August 2, 2012, from http://www.asyousow.org.csr

Corporate Social Responsibility Defined. Retrieved July 30, 2012, from http://www.businessearth.com

Covey, S. R., & Merrill, R. (2006). *The speed of trust: The one thing that changes everything.* New York, NY: The Free Press.

Coyle, J., Langley, C., & Gibson, B. Novack, R., & Bardi, E. (2013). *Supply chain management: A logistics perspective,* 9th edn. Mason, OH: South-Western.

Cuthbert, S. A. (2010). *Get rid of the performance review.* New York, NY: Business Plus, Hachette Book Group.

Dobler, D., Lee, L., & Burt, D. (1995). *Purchasing and supply management: Text and cases.* New York: McGraw-Hill.

Drucker, P. (1973). *Management: Tasks, responsibilities, practices.* New York, NY: Harper and Row Publishers.

Fortune, 1946, cited in Bowen H. R. (1953). *Social Responsibilities of the Businessman.* New York: Harper and Row, p. 44.

Follett, M. P. (1933). The Essentials of Leadership. In *Mary Parker Follett: Freedom and coordination.* London: Pitman Publishing, 1949, 47–60.

Friedman, T. L. (2006). *The world is flat.* New York, NY: Farrar, Straus, and Giroux.

Goleman, D. (1995). *Emotional intelligence.* New York, NY: Bantam Books.

Gordon, M., & Levin, M. (2009). Working with suppliers to achieve CSR goals. *Inside Supply Management,* 30–33.

Guze, T. (2011). *Average income in Japan 2010—Winter bonus time.* Retrieved May 29, 2011, from http://www.Withinjapan.com

Hill, Brad (2000). Assessing Variable Compensation Readiness. In Fay, C. H. (Ed.), *The executive handbook on compensation.* New York, NY: The Free Press.

Hirota et al. (2010). Corporate mission, corporate policies, and business outcomes: Evidence from Japan. *Management Decision 48*(7), pp. 1134–1153.

Hirota, S., Kubo, K., & Miyajima, H. (2007). *Does corporate culture matter? An empirical study of Japanese firms.* Tokyo, Japan: The Research Institute of Economy, Trade and Industry.

Jackson, I. A., & Nelson, J. (2004). *Profits with principles.* New York, NY: Doubleday.

Joseph, E., & Winston, B. (2005). A correlation of servant leadership, leader trust, and organizational trust. *Leadership and Organizational Development Journal 26*(1), pp. 6–22.

Kaplan, R., & Norton, D. P. (1996). *The Balanced scorecard: Translating strategy into action.* Cambridge, MA: HBS Press.

Karnani, A. (2010, August 22). *The case against corporate social responsibility.* Retrieved August 2, 2012, from http://online.wsj.com

Kerr, S. (1975). On the folly of rewarding A while hoping for B. *Academy of Management Journal 18,* December, pp. 769–783.

Kreps, T. J. (1940). Measurement of the Social Performance of Business. In *An investigation of concentration of economic power for the temporary national economic committee (Monograph 7).* Washington, D. C.: U. S. Government Printing Office.

Krisher, T. (2012). GM CEO says old culture still hinders change. *Associated Press,* August.

Likert, R. (1961). *New patterns of management.* New York, NY: McGraw-Hill Inc.

Matejka, K. J. (1991). *Why this horse won't drink: How to win and keep employee commitment.* New York, NY: AMACOM.

Mericle, K., & Kim, D. (2004). *Gainsharing and goals sharing: Aligning pay and strategic goals.* Westport, CT: Praeger Publishers.

Mintzberg, H. (2006). Communityship is the answer. *Financial Times Special Report—Business,* October 23.

Monczka, R., Handfield, R. Giunipero, L., & Patterson, J. (2011). *Purchasing and supply chain management,* 5th edn. Mason, OH: South-Western.

Narasimhan, R. , Kull, T., & Nahm, A. (2012). Alternative relationships among integrative beliefs, time-based manufacturing, and performance. *Journal of Operations and Production Management 32*(4), pp. 496–524.

Nelson, D., Moody, P. E., & Stegner, J. (2001). *The purchasing machine.* New York, NY: The Free Press.

Nonaka, I., & Takeuchi, H. (1995). *The knowledge creating company.* New York, NY: Oxford University Press.

Pascale, A., & Athos, A. (1981). The Art of Japanese Management. New York: Simon and Schuster.

Porter, M. E., & Kramer, M. (2006). Strategy and society. *Harvard Business Review 84*(12), pp. 78–92.

Porter, M. E. (1985). *Competitive advantage.* New York, NY: The Free Press.

Porter, L. W., & Lawler, E. E. (1968). *Managerial attitudes and performance.* Homewood, IL: Richard D. Irwin, Inc.

Prober, Larry M. (2000). EVA: A better financial reporting tool. *Pennsylvania CPA Journal,* Abstract, Fall.

Ross, D. (2011). *Introduction to supply chain management technologies,* 2nd edn. New York, NY: CRC Press.

Saban, K., & Mawhinney, J. (2010). Human collaboration: A key component to supply chain performance. *Journal of Applied Marketing Theory 1,* 32–44.

Schonberger, Richard J. (1982). *Japanese manufacturing techniques.* New York, NY: The Free Press.

Schuster, M. H. (2007). *Aligning compensation strategy.* Retrieved April 1, 2011, from http://www.jobfunctions.bnet.com

Senge, P. M. (1990). *The fifth discipline.* New York, NY: Doubleday.

Slegfried, M. (2012). Collaborating with the competition. *Inside Supply Management*, March.

Smith, Adam (1776). An Inquiry Into the Nature and Causes of the Wealth of Nations. Chicago: Encyclopedia Brittanica; William Benton Publisher, 1952.

Stets, J. E., & Burke, P. J. (2000). Identity theory and social identity theory. *Social Psychology Quarterly 63*(3), pp. 224–237.

Takeuchi, H., & Nonaka, I. (1986). The new product development game. *Harvard Business Review,* January/February, p. 139.

Time (1955). Management: The Scanlon plan. *Time LXVI*(13), September 26.

Value Chain Group (2012). http://www.value-chain.org/bptf/Value Chain Design/

Vickery, S., Jayaram, J., Droge, C., & Catalone, R. (2003). The effects of an integrative supply chain on customer service and financial performance. *Journal of Operations Management,* December, pp. 523–539.

Weber, M. (1987). Legitimate Authority and Bureaucracy. In Boone, L. E., & Bowen, D. (Ed.), *The great writings in management and organizational behavior,* 2nd edn. New York, NY: Random House.

Zingheim, P., & Schuster, J. (2007). What are key pay issues right now? *Compensation and Benefits Review,* May/June, pp. 51–55.

Index

OTHER TITLES IN OUR SUPPLY AND OPERATIONS MANAGEMENT COLLECTION

M. Johnny Rungtusanatham, Ohio State University Collection Editor

- *Production Line Efficiency: A Comprehensive Guide for Managers* by Sabry Shaaban and Sarah Hudson
- *Transforming US Army Supply Chains: Strategies for Management Innovation* by Greg Parlier
- *Design, Analysis and Optimization of Supply Chains: A System Dynamics Approach* by William Killingsworth
- *Supply Chain Planning and Analytics: The Right Product in the Right Place at the Right Time* by Gerald Feigin
- *Supply-Chain Survival in the Age of Globalization* by James A. Pope
- *Better Business Decisions: Using Cost Modeling For Procurement, Operations, and Supply Chain Professionals* by Victor Sower and Christopher Sower, Christopher
- *Supply Chain Risk Management: Tools for Analysis* by David Olson
- *Leading and Managing the Lean Management Process* by Gene Fliedner
- *Supply Chain Information Technology* by David Olson
- *Global Supply Chain Management* by Matt Drake
- *Managing Commodity Price Risk: A Supply Chain Perspective* by George A. Zsidisin and Janet Hartley
- *Improving Business Performance With Lean* by James Bradley
- *RFID for the Supply Chain and Operations Professional* by Pamela Zelbst, Pamela and Victor Sower
- *Insightful Quality: Beyond Continuous Improvement* by Victor Sower and Frank Fair
- *Sustainability Delivered: Designing Socially and Environmentally Responsible Supply Chains* by Madelaine Pullman and Margaret Sauter
- *Strategic Leadership of Portfolio and Project Management* by Timothy J. Kloppenborg and Laurence J. Laning
- *Sustainable Operations and Closed-Loop Supply Chains* by Gilvan Souza
- *Supply Chain Planning: Practical Frameworks for Superior Performance* by Matthew Liberatore, Matthew and Tan Miller

Announcing the Business Expert Press Digital Library

Concise E-books Business Students Need for Classroom and Research

This book can also be purchased in an e-book collection by your library as

- a one-time purchase,
- that is owned forever,
- allows for simultaneous readers,
- has no restrictions on printing, and
- can be downloaded as PDFs from within the library community.

Our digital library collections are a great solution to beat the rising cost of textbooks. e-books can be loaded into their course management systems or onto student's e-book readers.

The **Business Expert Press** digital libraries are very affordable, with no obligation to buy in future years. For more information, please visit **www.businessexpertpress.com/librarians**. To set up a trial in the United States, please contact **Adam Chesler** at *adam.chesler@businessexpertpress .com* for all other regions, contact **Nicole Lee** at *nicole.lee@igroupnet.com*.